FRIENDS AND NEIGHBOURS

Tom Kingscote-Davies

ISIS

LARGE PRINT

Oxford

First published in Great Britain 2006
by
The Book Guild Ltd.

Published in Large Print 2006 by ISIS Publishing Ltd.,
7 Centremead, Osney Mead, Oxford OX2 0ES
by arrangement with
The Book Guild Ltd.

British Library Cataloguing in Publication Data
Kingscote-Davies, Tom
    Friends and neighbours. – Large print ed.
    (Isis reminiscence series)
    1. Kingscote-Davies, Tom – Childhood and youth
    2. Farm life – Wales – Monmouthshire
    3. Large type books
    4. Monmouthshire (Wales) – Biography
    5. Monmouthshire (Wales) – Social life and
    customs – 20th century
    I. Title
    942.9'9083'092

ISBN-10 0–7531–9390–6 (hb)
ISBN-13 978–0–7531–9390–7 (hb)

ISBN 978–0–7531–9391–4 (pb)

Printed and bound in Great Britain by
T. J. International Ltd., Padstow, Cornwall

To Pauline, who was denied companionship and conversation whilst this manuscript was being prepared.

Contents

1. Hearsay — Not Memories 1
2. The Baptist Minister...........................4
3. Seats of Learning — One 11
4. The Old Moke................................23
5. The Sunday School Outing 30
6. Christmas on the Farm 46
7. William.....................................57
8. Haytime and Harvest.........................71
9. Chapels.....................................90
10. Grandfather's Farm 104
11. Cheese and Cider 131
12. The Fat Pig.................................141
13. Seats of Learning — Two.....................149
14. Seats of Learning — Three 161
15. The Hereford Bull 172
16. The Horse Show 184
17. Seats of Learning — Four.....................196

CHAPTER ONE

Hearsay — Not Memories

Old George. Now there was a character!

One of the first clear memories I have of my early childhood is of her rummaging amongst the straw and litter in the farmyard. I can still see her grey figure busily searching, or resting under the shade of the big ash tree which overhung the pond. Everyone was sad when the old grey-speckled Plymouth Rock hen died. She was reputed to be eight years old and was the pet of the farmyard.

Before this the details were hearsay. So how did it all start?

The farm stood at the top of a steep bank above a small tree-lined valley covered with brambles and hiding a brook which weaved and twisted through dingle and meadow to join the river Trothy. On the other side of the brook the ground rose sharply to the main road between Abergavenny and Ross.

From this highway a stone track led over a narrow bridge and up the hill to the farm. It was along this route that the district nurse rode her "sit-up-and-beg" bicycle in the early hours of one cold December morning.

Propping her bike against the yard wall, she turned off the water supply to the carbide lamp and knocked on the door. She bustled into the house, where a fire was blazing in the huge kitchen grate. Upstairs another fire was burning in one of the main bedrooms and the air was warm, in sharp contrast to the bleakness outside.

The deep stillness of the early hours was broken only by the occasional cry of some night bird. My brother Hal, barely three years old, slept peacefully but the adults were tense and anxious. The district nurse was calling for hot water from the coal-black kettle suspended from a hook over the roaring kitchen fire.

After what seemed an age to the waiting adults, the morning air was rent by a weak yell and another Sagittarian had arrived safely into a world which had been torn and ravaged by the most atrocious war in history. A month had elapsed since the cessation of hostilities and I gather that I was branded as something of a coward since I had arrived when the fighting was over. Whether or not I had taken some time in deciding to enter this world I don't know, but I was also called, by some people, "Doubting Thomas". I suspect, however, that this was due more to the family's strong religious leanings.

It appears that my brother was something of an experimentalist, particularly as regards one of the four elements of the ancient philosophers — namely fire. My mother and the nursemaid were out of the room for a few moments, leaving me asleep in the pram. Somehow my brother managed to out-manoeuvre the fireguard and lit a taper, which he applied to the blankets in the pram. Fortunately for me, wool is not readily inflammable and also it makes a most unpleasant smell when smouldering. This was readily detected by my mother, who arrived in time to stop the black oozy mess of wool from coming into contact with my tender baby skin.

I suppose I could say that my early demise was prevented by a sheep as a cellulosic fibre would have cooked me to a turn before help arrived.

The nurse, Doris, had left our home before my memory began to function. Perhaps she couldn't stand me as a baby since I have always had the reputation of being stubborn and obstinate which, according to the astrological charts, is in keeping with the Sagittarian character.

CHAPTER
TWO

The Baptist Minister

My family all worshipped as Nonconformists. My father was the organist in the local chapel, superintendent of the Sunday school and a trustee of the chapel.

It was not surprising, then, that we opened our doors to a Baptist minister. He was a widower and had just returned to England from New Zealand, where he had emigrated in the early part of the century.

Mr Cule was a true Welshman who had been brought up in the Rhondda Valley. He lived with us as far back as I can remember and I loved him dearly. He was a short, stocky man dressed in clerical black. His clerical collar and false shirt cuffs were made of white celluloid and were always sparkling white since they only needed sponging daily with a damp cloth.

He had a white goatee beard and a white moustache and was probably in his early seventies when he came to us. Although he had two rooms for his own use, he was really one of the family and, as I sat beside him, he recounted wondrous stories of his travels to far-off lands. I never tired of his tales of man-eating sharks following the ship or of the Maoris in New Zealand.

A local term in Monmouthshire when a white mould appeared on perishable foodstuffs was to say that they were "fausty". One day at dinner I had been studying Mr Cule with great intensity and, looking at his white beard, I burst out with, "Mr Cule, why have you gone fausty?" This seemed to cause a great deal of amusement amongst the family.

Mr Cule had brought with him an Edison Bell phonograph and a rare collection of one hundred and forty cylindrical records. Since wireless was practically unheard of in that part of the country, this provided a good source of entertainment. Records and books of many titles were stacked neatly on shelves in the study that was Mr Cule's domain. On winter evenings it was a great treat to sit in the snug study and listen to the phonograph with its huge trumpet horn.

"Mr Cule, can we have the phonograph on tonight, please?" With pleading eyes the question was put.

"You must ask your daddy if you can stay up."

"Daddy, can we listen to the phonograph? Please, just this once."

Some humming and hawing.

"W-e-ll, all right, but to bed straight away afterwards."

Great excitement! Sweaty little hands got in the way but were eager to help.

"Don't you drop those records or they'll break."

I would sit patiently whilst the grown-ups listened to orchestral renderings of "The Merry Widow", "The Boys of the Old Brigade", "Marching Through

Georgia" or vocal renderings of Caruso, Harry Lauder singing "Breakfast in Bed", or Billy Williams with "Wait Till I'm as Old as Father".

My great moments were to come but impatience at last got the upper hand.

"Mr Cule, when can we have 'Pussy Cat Rag'?" Much pestering and then,

> I've got an old maid sister,
> Who's crazy over cats,
> She wears her hair in paper down, Cause she's
>   afraid of rats,
> She's got the neighbours talking,
> And they don't think she's right,
> For you can hear her calling cats,
> At any time of night . . .
> "Pussy, Pussy, Pussy, Pussy, Pussy . . ."

and so on, until the scratching denoted the end of the record.

"That was lovely — can we hear it once more?"

And then "Pussy Cat Rag" was on the air again.

"I think it's time the boys were in bed," said my father.

"But we haven't heard 'Willie Winkle' yet," chorused my brother and I.

"Well, all right, but then to bed."

Scratch, scratch, then,

> Willie Winkle played a wrinkle on his fiddle-dee-
>   dee,

Dolly Dimple sweet and simple said "Oh play it
   for me",
Then a feeling comes a-stealing,
What does this melody say?
"It sounds silly but go on, Willy,
Let me hear you pla-a-aay".
Rum-tum-tum-tum-tum-ta-tiddle,
Was the tune he played upon his fiddle . . .

Then with the candle flame flickering in the draughty passage, up the stairs to bed we went. Sleepyhead, soft pillow and dreams of "Pussy Cat Rag" and "Willie Winkle".

Mr Cule had also brought with him a contraption called a cabinet bath. When set up, this formed a cube of waterproof material on a strong wire framework. In the top was a hole through which the head protruded to enable the user to breathe comfortably, and there was a door in the front which could be fastened to retain the heat. A special chair like a lavatory seat was placed inside, and under the chair was a small stove which burnt methylated spirits. It was, in effect, a portable Turkish bath.

    Whenever Mr Cule had a cold he would try to effect a cure by sweating it out in the cabinet and then have a hipbath in front of the fire.

    My father used to fasten the door of the cabinet and arrange to return in ten minutes to let Mr Cule out, by which time the heat in the cabinet would have become quite intense. On one occasion something of a drama arose. My father became engrossed in one of his many jobs about the farm and forgot about the time. My mother, meanwhile, suddenly became aware of urgent and agonised cries for help.

"Ed, Ed, let me out, let me out."

She considered it quite improper for her to answer the anguished call and rushed out to find my father whilst the urgent pleas continued with increasing intensity.

My father, after what must have seemed an aeon of time to Mr Cule, finally came to the rescue, half expecting to find a grease spot where once Mr Cule had sat. He rapidly undid the cabinet door and a fatigued, lobster-red figure staggered forth. Needless to say, this was not allowed to occur again.

Occasionally Mr Cule would go away for a few days to hold services in his home town in the Rhondda and I would be forlornly awaiting his return to play games with me once again. He had a knack of protruding his front teeth in such a way that the mild-mannered minister became a ferocious Mr Hyde. With his eyes popping out like chapel hat pegs, he would chase me until I was petrified with terror. A moment or two to recover then, "Do it again, Mr Cule." What a glutton I was for punishment!

On his return he would bring us a gift and on one memorable occasion this was a fountain pen. As this was still the steel nib age, how we treasured this gift and promised not to disturb him in future when he was preparing his sermons.

Each Tuesday was market day in Abergavenny and when he returned from his weekly visit to town we were assured of a packet of Nestlé's milk chocolate each. My brother usually ate his at one go but, for some unaccountable reason, I would hoard mine, like a squirrel, in a tin tea canister which was kept high up on a corner of the mantelshelf.

My brother was apt to raid my supplies and this provoked a violent reaction on my part.

Mr Cule used to tell me amusing stories but I didn't realise at the time that some of them had more than one possible interpretation. I have thought since that he may have not realised it either. For example:

There were two elderly spinsters, one of whom was rather deaf. They attended the village church regularly and during the week a new vicar had taken up his post. The two ladies were looking forward to meeting him but the deaf one had a cold and couldn't leave the house. The other called to see him. When she returned home her sister asked, "What is the new vicar like?"

"Oh, he's very pleasant but talks rather loudly."

"What did you say, dear?"

"I said he talks rather loudly."

"Sorry, dear, I didn't catch what you said."

"Bawls like a bull."

"Has he!"

When Mr Cule returned to England he had left behind a son who was also a minister of the Baptist Church in New Zealand. When I was nine years old Mr Cule decided to return there to spend the rest of his years with his son and family. He was then eighty years of age.

One dismal morning after breakfast I tenderly kissed his white-whiskered cheek, whispered goodbye, and rushed off to school with tears of sorrow rushing down my face.

In my childish way I couldn't understand why his son and grandchildren should want to take him away when my need was so much greater.

In my prayers for long afterwards I asked God to send him back to me. I knew deep in my heart that these prayers could not be answered but I did have long letters telling me of his life far away across the waters.

CHAPTER
THREE

Seats of Learning — One

The time had now come for me to start my schooling and it was with mixed feelings that I set off one morning with my brother on the mile-long walk to the school.

It was in an isolated position on the side of a hill about a half a mile from the nearest hamlet, which boasted a small general stores, a blacksmith's and carpenter's shop and a few houses, not to mention the post office with its red cast iron post box set into the side of a stone wall.

From the school playground there was a magnificent view across unspoilt countryside to the Skirrid, Blorange and Sugarloaf mountains. On one side they towered over the steep valleys leading to the industrial area of Monmouthshire and on the other to the Brecon Beacons. At times these mountains were coloured purple by distance.

The school was stone-built and consisted of one large lofty room with a smaller room leading off. This accommodated the infant class and was where I first began to count with the aid of beads on wires stretched between a wooden frame.

The school house was built on to the side of the school and was home of the two spinster ladies who tried to instil some learning into the motley collection of children who attended the school. A well with a pump provided water for all our needs. The tarmacadam playground was surrounded by a wall built against the side of the hill. At the top of the playground stood the closets and the segregation of the sexes was discreetly maintained by a high dividing wall between "BOYS" and "GIRLS".

Whenever nature's call needed answering the request was always the same. Baby talk was forgotten now.

"Please, Miss, I want to go to the 'Top'."

"Are you sure, Reggie? You only went a short while ago."

"Yes, Miss."

"Well, go on then and hurry up."

Desks creak, small hob-nailed boots clump across the wooden floor, doors bang, a scurry of feet to the "Top", a brief interval of silence and then the sound of boots sliding down the steep slope of the playground.

The pupils came from diverse types of homes. There were the children of labourers, roadmen, well-to-do farmers and the very poor. All the children, with the exception of one family, took their lunches to school in their satchels. The exception was a large family but a very cheerful one. The brothers and sisters were always laughing and smiling but they were as poor as church mice and trudged to school, in all weathers, across the fields from the other side of the Greig hill. For these children the mistresses prepared, each day, large slabs of corned beef sandwiches. Their diet was consistent — corned beef today, tomorrow, next week, next month for as long as I knew them. The memory of Reggie with his flaming red hair, scoffing corned beef with bread and margarine, is still vividly in my mind. He would wipe the crumbs out of the way of his huge grin and pop around to the pump to wash down the remnants with well-water.

Whilst I was in the infant class our teacher was involved in some special duties in the large classroom one day and we were left to amuse ourselves with crayons and coloured chalks. After some time I became rather bored with this and thought that it was time that the afternoon took on a more lively atmosphere.

I decided that I would be a savage lion on the rampage and started to put this idea into effect. Uttering what I imagined to be blood-curdling roars, I ran amok, biting all the other children on their arms. Not viciously but sufficient to raise screams of alarm and to induce terror into my young classmates.

The din became deafening until it was brought to an abrupt end by the appearance of one severe-looking teacher in the doorway.

"What's all this noise about?"

"Please, Miss, he bit me."

"Who bit you?"

"He did, Miss."

A dozen accusing fingers pointed at me. By now all savagery had melted from me like hailstones on the hot summer ground. In place of the roaring lion stood a pale-faced, pathetic little boy.

"You naughty boy. Why did you do this? You're nothing but a little savage. Just wait until your parents know about this."

I wished fervently that the ground would open and swallow me up. No-one would speak to me or come near me. I was an outcast. Such misery was almost beyond endurance. Would things ever be the same again?

After what seemed the longest afternoon ever, it was time to go home. But this was not the end of the matter, for my brother reprimanded me all the way home and then gave a full account of my behaviour to my father and mother. For once I was truly glad to go to bed and welcomed the oblivion of sleep.

The hill behind the school was covered with dense bracken during the summer months and the favourite game during the lunch hour was "fox and hounds". One boy would be the "fox" and would set off for his hide in the bracken. Others would be huntsmen and the rest the hounds.

"Taraa, taraa," sounded the make-believe horns.

A loud yelping of human dogs and the hunt was on. Eventually the "fox" broke cover and a crescendo of noise erupted.

"Tally Ho! Tally Ho!"

If the "fox" was the fastest runner he usually got away before the bell sounded. If not, the "hounds" would eventually catch up and the "fox" would sink panting to the ground, his flannel shirt soaking with sweat after his exertions in the mid-day sun.

Then would follow a mad dash to the pump for gulps of refreshing well water. One boy would man the pump whilst the rest held their mouths under the steadily gushing stream. The more adventuresome, such as red-headed Reggie, put their whole heads in the stream.

I had been told that I mustn't do this on any account since such terrible afflictions as meningitis or "water-on-the-brain" must surely result. This made sense to me at five years of age particularly as Mr Cule had told me about an incident concerning his travels in the Arctic Circle.

According to his story, the party were suddenly faced by a polar bear. The hunter with them fired his muzzle loader and missed. When he came to reload he found that he had run out of shot, so he broke off a sharp icicle and pushed it down the barrel. This time he took careful aim, fired, and the icicle penetrated the bear's scull. The icicle melted and the bear died from "water-on-the-brain". My brother, however, ignored all this advice and with great bravado, underwent the baptism.

During my stay at this school my ears picked up a number of new words. Amongst these were two four-letter words which I didn't understand and which I tried out on my mother when I got home.

She was horrified and told me quietly that such words were very rude and that I should never use them again. I could see that she was very upset by my behaviour, although quite innocent, and I resolved never to use them again.

From the school playground I could see my grandparents' farm in the far distance. I spent many happy days there during the school holidays and often I wished that I could be there instead of at school.

One lovely summer day my grandmother arrived with her pony and trap during the mid-day break to take me home. To my surprise I was told that I was to go with her on a short visit which she was making to her cousin in one of the industrial towns of Monmouthshire. We were driven into Abergavenny, where we took a train for Ebbw Vale.

I saw a train perhaps two or three times a year and to actually ride in one was indeed a treat. The train huffed and puffed its way up through Gilwern and along the side of the steep valley, through the tunnel to emerge again before entering Brynmawr station. Then it went on and over a high viaduct to Ebbw Vale. From there the line continued to Merthyr.

There was a song which we used to sing to the tune of "Mochin Du":

On the Brecon-Merthyr line
There's an engine number nine,
Which by its own power
Will go five miles an hour.
Did you ever see,
Did you ever see,
Did you ever see,
Such a funny thing before.

When we arrived at our relatives' home we were given an affectionate welcome. Two particular memories of this visit stick in my mind.

The man of the house just sat in the same chair in the same corner of the room. He was there when I went to bed at night and he was there when I got up in the morning, just as though he was part of the furniture. He spoke but little and I was puzzled and somewhat frightened of him. This was the period of industrial depression in the 1920s and unemployment was rife in this part of Monmouthshire. He was a steel worker and had been unemployed for some years but it was not until I was much older that I realised how a long period of unemployment could affect a man physically and mentally and make him withdraw into a world of his own.

Whilst on this visit I was out walking with my grandmother and her cousin. By chance, we were alongside the railway line when a colliers' train halted. A multitude of black faces with windows of pearly white teeth peered out of the carriages. These miners were on their way home after the early day shift. There were not any pit-head baths in those days and each miner took home the day's coal dust, which he removed in a hip-bath in front of the kitchen fire.

"Look at all those black boys!" exclaimed my grandmother. "Wouldn't you like to take one home with you?"

"Oh! Yes please," said I, fully expecting my wish to be granted. Alas I was to be disappointed. We returned from our walk with me blubbering like a child crying for the moon.

After a few days I was not sorry to leave the land of slag heaps and coal dust for the green fields of the farm again, even if it did mean a return to school.

Our childish, unenlightened minds were filled with apprehension at the news that all the pupils were to be examined by the school doctor. Thus when the time came for him to make his periodic visit the excuses for not going to school that day were many and varied.

"I don't feel like going to school today, I feel sick," I told my mother.

"But the doctor is coming today."

"Yes, I know."

"You don't feel feverish," said she, feeling my forehead. "Have you been eating green apples?"

"I haven't touched them."

"Well, there doesn't seem to be much wrong with you. Now hurry up or you'll be late for school."

I was bundled off with my brother, who didn't relish the day ahead either. To make up the time we jog-trotted most of the way. However, as is often the case, the fear of the unknown was much worse than coming to grips with reality. The doctor was an understanding, kindly soul and, after a quick appraisal of my physical status, the meeting was quickly ended.

On the other hand, my brother had a much more interesting experience which pricked my curiosity in no small way and made me profoundly jealous. He told me that he had been examined in company with the older girls, who were in various stages of undress.

"Did they undress in front of you?" I asked the question, eyes wide with astonishment.

"Yes, of course."

"What do they wear?" was all I could think of to ask him.

"Oh! Just flannel vests and baggy blue bloomers."

And I had missed it all! There seemed to be no justice in this world.

Even at such a tender age something had stirred within me, for I had been developing a bit of a crush on blue-eyed Edith, one of several daughters of a neighbouring farmer, who used to walk home with us for part of the way. I enjoyed kissing her goodbye at the stile where our ways parted.

And I had that day missed the opportunity of getting to know her better by having a glimpse of her flannel vest and blue bloomers. How intimate that would have been! A lost opportunity and all because of some inefficient organisation by teachers and doctor.

My fretting did not last long. Even the parting kisses were soon forgotten since within a couple of minutes we arrived at the cottage of my father's old aunt and uncle, where the void of unrequited love was promptly filled with Welsh cakes and lemonade.

One day, after our usual snack of lemonade and cakes, we were dawdling on our last leg of the homeward journey. At intervals along the road heaps of stone chippings and large barrels of a sticky black mess had been deposited. This was our first encounter with coal tar, apart from that which oozed out of lumps of coal in the firegrate. The dusty stone surface was to disappear for ever and a tarred surface was to take its place. The Ross road would never be the same again.

"Doan know what them council blokes be thinking of," said the locals. "How'd they think th'osses be gwawn keep their foothold in frosty weather?"

But buses and the odd motorcar were becoming more frequent along this road and a smoother surface was necessary. So, 'osses notwithstanding, progress was on the march.

It wasn't just the horses that the tar was to bother. It bothered my mother too, for on the day that it first appeared on the scene we thought that it was fine stuff to play with. The result of our experiments was that we became smothered with the black goo — hands, faces and clothes. We tried to remove it by washing in the little brook by the bridge on the track to the farm. To our horror we found that water wasn't quite the universal solvent we had supposed it to be and we walked sheepishly into the house, to be greeted with a look of dismay and disbelief from our mother. "What on earth have you been doing? You stupid little monkeys!" she cried.

There followed a thorough scolding and a few well-deserved slaps. Later, after much rubbing with home-made lard, our skin was at last clean and we were packed off to bed so that the lesson would not be forgotten. After that, tar was strictly for the roads.

Morning school always began with prayers and, to the accompaniment of the piano, we would give full vent to "All things bright and beautiful".

The Lord's Prayer was chanted mechanically by the older pupils and I was learning it. A bigger boy, Ron James, stood next to me most mornings. He had a loud voice and I used to follow him closely.

"Our Father which chart in Heaven," he used to say.

One evening I was sitting by the fire and I told Mr Cule that I knew the Lord's Prayer.

"That's good," he said. "Say it to me."

"Our Father which chart in Heaven," I started.

"No, no it isn't 'which chart', it's 'which art'," said Mr Cule.

"It isn't," I said. Then a heated argument followed.

"Ron James says 'which chart' and he should know," I said.

Why Ron James should be a greater authority on religious matters than Mr Cule, who was a Baptist minister, I couldn't imagine, but I was convinced at the time that this was so.

My two years at this school were carefree, but whether I learned much is open to question.

FRIENDS AND NEIGHBOURS

We then moved to South Monmouthshire, where we had to acclimatise ourselves to new surroundings and to make new friends, but that is another story.

CHAPTER
FOUR

The Old Moke

Neddy, our donkey, was a well-established farmyard pet for as long as I can remember. She had a dingy grey coat and a thin wispy tail. She was bought for "the boys", as my brother and I were usually referred to.

My earliest recollections of Neddy are from old photographs. There is a snapshot of me sitting on her broad back, perched like a pimple on a haystack. My brother, six years old, standing bolt upright like a pouter pigeon and looking very proud and responsible, is holding the reins.

We used to ride the old moke bareback, at least we did when she was in the mood for us to do so. She was normally very docile but, at times, very stubborn. On one occasion I was on her back, trying to get her to move, but she was in one of her obstinate moods. My brother Hal and Mr Cule were slapping her and trying to get her mobile.

"Git up, you idiot. Gee-up, you stubborn old ass."

She dug her heels in and shifted her centre of gravity to her rear.

"Come on, old girl, gee-up." But no amount of coaxing had any effect either.

"Leave her to me," said Mr Cule.

He walked across to the hedge and came back with a thick stick. One sharp whack across her rump had a most explosive effect. Jet propulsion had not been thought of in those days but my guess is that Neddy was its first exponent.

She started forward so suddenly that, whilst at one moment I was sitting comfortably, the next I was momentarily suspended in thin air. The force of gravity being what it is, my young bottom and Mother Earth were pushing each other with equal intensity, and I'm sure she didn't find the experience as painful an I did.

"All right bach, don't cry. Are you hurt?" asked Mr Cule. Both my companions looked anxiously at me and then at the old moke. She had stopped after her sudden rush and was studying the scene with a reproachful look. I dusted down my linen shorts and made off for the house.

I had one other mishap with Neddy a year or so later. At the bottom of one of the fields was a dingle formed by an old Roman road. A low hedge skirted the field and on the other side of it the ground fell sharply to the sunken roadway, now overgrown with bushes and nettles. Neddy was grazing near the hedge as I went over to speak to her. She must have been in one of her moods for she waited until I was near her rear quarters then, with beautiful timing, she lashed out with her hind legs, catching me in the stomach and lifting me clean over the hedge and into the roadway below.

I picked myself up from the brambles and nettles, pricked and nettled in more ways than one, but fortunately none the worse for wear.

We had a complete set of harness and a donkey cart for Neddy. In company with the sons and two daughters of the neighbouring farmer, we would harness her up and go for a short trip on a fine summer evening.

The route usually taken was along the Ross road for about a half a mile to the cottage of our great-aunt and uncle, returning along a narrow lane until we reached a gate leading into the fields at the other end of the farm, then a merry trot across the fields to the farmyard.

It was just as well that Neddy was docile. Although lorries and buses were very few and far between at that time and the horse-drawn wagon and dray were the principal means of transporting goods apart from the railways, traction engines drawing long trailers were sometimes seen. These steaming, belching monsters clanked remorselessly along, their huge iron wheels on the stone road adding their share of noise to the din. Yet, in their own way, they were beautiful monsters, with the brassworks gleaming from the spit and polish lovingly bestowed upon them by their drivers.

Neddy was not unduly worried by this breed of iron horse and, looking neither to right nor left and flicking her long pointed ears, would trot on, drawing her load of exuberant youngsters. Indeed, when she put her mind to it, she could outpace this man-made beast of burden and leave it well behind.

On our arrival at the old stone cottage with its picturesque garden ablaze with summer flowers and the deep blue clematis climbing over the porch, the old couple gave us a royal welcome.

"So you be out for a ride eh?" said my uncle, who was a short, stocky man with a big white beard. "You stay and mind the moke while I see what your aunt has got indoors."

Then they both came out with trays of Welsh cakes and lemonade.

Whilst we were busily cramming the Welsh cakes down and swilling round the crumbs with lemonade, my aunt disappeared into the house and came back a moment or two later with some lumps of white sugar.

"Here you are, Neddy," she said, holding out a lump in the palm of her hand. Neddy gently fumbled the sugar into her mouth with her thick lips and munched away. Then she nuzzled my aunt's arm for more. After several more lumps she was impatient to be away.

All scrambled back into the cart, a flick of the reins and we were off.

"Goodbye, my dears," and two gnarled hands waved us off.

"Goodbye," we all chorused, and turned the corner into the lane.

The air of the summer evening was heavy with the scent of honeysuckle. A blackbird flitted from bush to bush at the sound of our approach, whilst the bleating of sheep and the lowing of cattle could be heard in the distance.

"Clippety-clop, clippety-clop" went Neddy's hooves on the dusty road. My brother sat up front holding the reins, back straight and looking full of importance. For an eight-year-old this was some responsibility!

Despite what people say, donkeys are not stupid but rather self-willed. As soon as we reached the gate to the field leading to home, she stopped; but as soon as the gate was opened and we were through it, she had to be tightly reined in until the gate was fastened and we were all safely aboard again. Then we were off at a steady canter, Neddy glad to be nearing home and we sorry that our little excursion was nearly over.

Ahead of us peewits with their plaintive cries were flitting out of the way and, with a rush of wings, a covey of partridges broke cover and glided over the hedge into the next field. The cart swayed and bumped over the rough ground. As we sat on the wooden seats our small bodies were shaken this way and that. But who cared? We were having fun.

Then into the field at the back of the barn, through the gate and under the big elm trees skirting the rickyard by the pond, and we were home. Out of the cart, we rushed into the house for some sugar lumps.

"Good girl Neddy, lovely old Neddy, you've earned your sugar."

Neddy waited patiently whilst she was taken out of the shafts and unharnessed, then, with a loud "hee-haw", she kicked her hind legs into the air and galloped off into the field to join the horses.

Saying goodnight to our young friends, we watched them set off down the "field-below-the-house" to their own home. The black stockings of the two girls blended with the gathering dusk until they themselves seemed to be floating through the mist now beginning to rise from the ground.

Some years later we moved to another farm in South Monmouthshire, taking all our stock, including Neddy, with us. She soon became a firm favourite with the local children, who used to feed her carrots from their cottage gardens.

My father had bought a large pony, whom we named Kitty, when we moved to the new farm. She was a beautiful sleek-coated creature and could move like the wind. Drawing a tub with two passengers, she could cover the seven miles into Abergavenny in half-an-hour. She also had a fiery temper and, at times, was difficult to control.

Kitty and Neddy, despite their different temperaments, became firm and inseparable friends. They were always to be seen together. One morning, after breakfast, my father went out to check the stock. In the field Neddy was lying prostrate and Kitty was standing over her, head down and motionless.

Poor old Neddy had drawn her last breath. The magpies had got there before us and had pecked out her eyes. This was in accordance with the nature of wild creatures but to me it was a pathetic sight.

That same day my father dug a grave at the bottom of the field where the ground was softer. He harnessed one of the cart-horses and with chains dragged the lifeless grey body to the pit. Kitty followed the procession a few yards in the rear, with head held low, and stood by the side of the pit whilst my father began to shovel in the earth. When the body was finally covered she tossed her head and, neighing wildly, dashed to the furthermost corner of the field, where she remained motionless. My father gathered up his tools and walked sadly back to the house.

Never again would we hear that raucous braying. A dear old friend had left us. She was forty years of age.

CHAPTER
FIVE

The Sunday School Outing

Each summer when the days were long and the weather was settled, the annual Sunday school trip to the seaside took place. We travelled by charabanc or coach, and to accommodate the children, their parents and friends, two coaches were needed. In fact the outing was an excuse for the young to forget school and for the adults to down tools and join the spree.

For days before, the air was crackling with excitement; we saw the sea but once a year and this was a day to be remembered and savoured to the full.

Finally the great day arrived and my parents and all the other farmers were up at crack of dawn, for there was much to be done before joining the coach party at eight o'clock. There were cows to be milked, the milk to be separated into cream and skimmed milk, poultry to be fed and stock checked. Then there was the great flurry of activity getting ready in Sunday best, sandwiches to be packed to sustain us on the journey and breakfast to be taken.

My brother and I needed no urging to leave our comfortable feather beds. In fact we had been wide awake since daybreak, tingling with excitement. It would have been small wonder if we had put on our trousers back to front. Our small fingers fumbled impatiently with our shoe laces and it seemed as if we would never be off.

"Have you washed your faces?" called my mother. "Let me see your hands."

We held out our hands for inspection.

"They're still grubby. You can't go out like that. Go and give them a jolly good scrub," said my mother impatiently.

Reluctantly we left to do so. This was a waste of time if ever there was. With all the water where we were going, it seemed so unnecessary to go to such extremes.

"Where are my stockings?" called my father from the top of the stairs.

My poor harassed mother was almost beside herself since she was trying to get ready at the same time as keeping an eye on the rest of the family. At last we were ready and the key was turning in the lock when someone shouted anxiously, "Have we got the sandwiches?"

A feverish search through the carrier bag produced the sandwiches, so we were assured that starvation wasn't imminent. With a final word to Sharp, the Welsh collie, to guard the house until our return, we were on our way.

We all met at the chapel. When we arrived excited groups were already gathered waiting for the coaches. It was a beautiful summer morning with a clear blue sky and no cloud to mar the promise of a lovely day. The birds were in full voice; yellowhammers flitted along the hedgerows, whilst from the distance came the staccato chatter of a magpie and the cheeky call of a jay.

My father, who was Superintendent of the Sunday school, was busy checking the list. What a disappointment if anyone should be left behind!

Suddenly a loud shout came from the children, "Here they come, here they come," as the two coaches appeared along the road from Abergavenny.

All scrambled aboard and, after a final check to see that no-one was missing, we were off.

Amongst the party were two old men who had never seen the sea: Farmer Bailly, who had, even at his great age, a mop of ginger hair and a large bushy ginger beard, and John Pryce, who had not been further afield than the local market towns. In their quaint dress they looked a most comical pair. It was obvious from the start that they were out to enjoy themselves and that they were going to make this a day of days.

Farmer Bailly was a rough fellow. On market days he usually got drunk in the Abergavenny pubs and on the local bus on the homeward journey his loud conversation with his cronies was crude, to say the least. My grandmother was most disgusted by his behaviour and lectured my grandfather very severely about associating with him.

The coaches made their way through Abergavenny and on to Usk, where we caught our glimpse of the river which gives its name to the ancient town with the Norman castle.

"Look at the river, isn't it big," chorused the children. "Ooh! Isn't it lovely!"

We were used to the small brook which ran through the farm and to see what, to us, was a wide, wide expanse of water with the sunlight making each drop a sparkling crystal as it flowed over the rapids, was indeed a lovely sight.

On again to Newport. What a big town, no buildings like this in Aber. Then on towards Cardiff. Between Newport and Cardiff the Bristol Channel appeared before our very eyes. What a shout that produced.

"The sea, the sea," went up the cry, and all the little ones stood on tip-toe so as not to miss a moment of this glorious sight.

"Just look at that big ship," cried one boy, and all eyes were directed along the line of the pointing finger. There she was, steaming majestically up the channel to Newport docks.

The drive along Cardiff's Queen Street was a treat in itself. The clanging, swaying trams going about their everyday business brought gasps of awe as these monsters charged their way through the multitude of cabs, cars and horsedrawn vehicles. And the buildings were even more ornate and bigger than those of Newport!

"I'm hungry — what have we got to eat? Can I have a sandwich please?" Sandwiches of home-cured ham and home-made cheese were produced and quickly eaten.

The journey passed quickly with so many new and interesting sights to occupy our attention. At length we topped the rise and there, before our very eyes, was the sea. The salty tang set nostrils twitching and the earlier chatter of the magpie near the chapel was now replaced by the screaming of the gulls planing over the vast expanse of water.

John Pryce stood spellbound at the sight of so much water. His first sight of the sea seemed to have made him bereft of his powers of speech. At last he recovered himself and burst out with, "Look at all that water! Never sin such a pond in all me life. Dang me, I nivver thought it would be like this."

The coaches disgorged their human cargo. Arms and legs were stretched and flexed after the long journey. One young tot clutched her mother's skirt and tugged urgently, her shrill voice crying, "Mamma, I want to go somewhere."

"Hush! Not so loud — can't you wait a few minutes?"

"No Mamma, it's now."

My father was just able to remind everyone where to assemble for the lunch which had been arranged, before mother and child hastily left to find a private outcrop of rock.

People split up into small parties of families and friends and went their own ways to explore the wonders of the seashore. John Pryce and Farmer Bailly hurried off to the nearest pub to sample the local brew.

"Can we have a ride on the donkeys?"

Hal and I had decided that this was a most essential part of the trip so, in company with our other young friends, we paid over our coppers, and mounting our steeds, urged them into a trot. The man in charge huffed and puffed alongside in the blazing sun, bare-footed and bored but, no doubt, thinking of the money he was raking in from us.

There were a few people bathing and we were allowed to take off our shoes and stockings and paddle. To us this was quite daring as we ventured in up to our knees, shrieking with a mixture of delight and terror as each wave threatened to soak our trousers. Some of the older women and mothers very sedately took off their shoes and stockings to paddle. The excuse was that the salt water was good for their corns. Skirts were held at knee height out of the water's reach but occasionally they were frantically raised higher when a larger wave came along, revealing a glimpse of elastic-bottomed blue bloomers. Very daring this! Shrieks of laughter accompanied this performance.

Miss Pritchard and Mrs Evans sat on a rock, looking down their noses at such frivolity. But their eyes almost popped out of their sockets when they saw Elsie Thomas emerge from a bathing hut swathed in a voluminous bathing suit.

"She's a flighty piece she is," said Miss Pritchard. "A proper hussy — fancy exposing her body like that. She'll come to no good, will she."

"I can't think what her parents are thinking of, letting her carry on like this," agreed Mrs Evans. "But have you heard that her sister Blodwen is to be married next week?"

"Next week? No, I didn't know about that. Sudden like, isn't it? Does she have to be?"

"No, no, I don't think it's anything like that," said Mrs Evans.

Meanwhile, Elsie, unaware of the deep interest in her and her family, was having the time of her life wallowing in the water. This was much better than being cramped up in a hip-bath in front of the kitchen fire after all the others had gone to bed.

The Brownie box cameras were much in use.

"Come on, Johnnie, stand next to Marion while I take your picture," shouted Auntie May above the general din of merriment. "We must have some snaps of the outing."

Johnnie and Marion stood side by side like two small soldiers, with wide grins on their faces.

"There, I hope it comes out all right, it will be nice for the album," exclaimed Auntie May.

The morning was slipping by and with all the excitement and donkey riding and paddling, the sea air had caused us to develop ravenous appetites, so the groups of trippers started to drift away from the beach to make their way to the restaurant for lunch.

The ice-cream cart caused some trouble on the way.

"Can I have a cornet, Mamma?" yelled one frustrated youngster.

"No, indeed you can't. It will spoil your dinner."

"But I never have an ice-cream."

"You can have one after dinner."

"Why not now?"

"After dinner."

Child tugged one way, mother tugged the other and, being stronger, won the day.

All filed into the large room and seated themselves at long tables. Some looked very self-conscious and uncomfortable in their new surroundings away from their home tables. John Pryce and Farmer Bailly, however, had evidently had a good morning. True, they had been near, very near, liquid, but not sea water, and the local brew had swept away any inhibitions they might have had. Farmer's raucous cackling could be heard above everyone else.

The waitresses whisked around the room dispensing plates of shop ham and tongue and salad to all the hungry trippers. I was fascinated to see how Farmer found the gap in his enormous whiskers through which he pushed large forkfuls of the food. This was shovelled around as if he was mucking out his cow-shed.

The meal was delicious.

"Gosh! This shop ham is nice — makes a change from the home-cured," said I, not realising how lucky I was to be able to have home-cured any day of the week. Townsfolk were prepared to pay what seemed to me enormous prices for home-cured ham.

The cleared plates were whipped away, to be replaced by dishes of blancmange with a cherry atop, and the whole lot was washed down with large quantities of lemonade.

"Pity we bent got any beer," said Farmer in a loud voice.

Hunger staunched, we were ready to be on the move again. It was decided that our group would visit Cold Knap and then return to the pleasure beach to take a boat trip and enjoy the fun of the fair. Cold Knap was completely different from the sandy beach where we had paddled and ridden the donkeys in the morning. It was a mass of smooth pebbles. Round, flat, oval, but as smooth as a baby's bottom.

Farmer Bailly and John Pryce were already there. Old John was almost overcome by the sight of all those pebbles. He was stuffing them in his pockets as though he hadn't a moment to spare and shouting at Farmer to do the same.

"Come on, Farmer, tek some 'ome wi yuh," he urged. "Look 'ow smooth they be, they'll do to sharpen yuh razor."

His pockets were bulging and he was so loaded with the weight that he waddled from side to side as he walked.

We later saw Farmer and John walking along the sea front. Whenever a pretty girl passed them, Farmer turned his head, gave her a saucy wink and said, "'ow be you, me lov?"

"Stop it, stop it, Bailly," pleaded old John. "You'll get us info trouble."

"Poof," said Farmer, "we be out for the day."

"Hello, me luv," he said to the next girl he saw.

"Be careful, Farmer, there's a policeman over there. We don't want to be run in," said John.

"Who cares," replied Farmer. "Let's have some fun."

"But who be going to feed my pigs and cows and do the milking if I gets landed in jail?" pleaded John.

Farmer was spreading his wings in no mean way in his old age. Despite the new and exciting experiences which old John was having, I fancied that it would be a relief to him to get back to the sanctuary of his own farm.

The tide was now well in and the pleasure boats were tied up waiting to take visitors for a trip around the bay. Old John had been looking rather puzzled by the appearance of this additional large quantity of water.

"Where be all this water come from?" he asked. "We bent 'ad any rain all mornin' but this 'ere pond be got bigger and bigger."

He looked thoroughly confused by it all.

Our small party walked gingerly down the landing stage towards the boat, the children clutched tightly by the hand for fear they would fall in the sea. Then there was the horrifying experience of clambering over the side of the boat, but the seamen lent helping hands to the awkward landlubbers.

"Come on, missus — up you come, mind yer skirt."

Mrs Evans and her spinster friend, Miss Pritchard, had been persuaded to come on the trip and they approached the problem of boarding with some trepidation. As a burly boatman grabbed Miss Pritchard's arm and hauled her aboard, her leg came into view to her knee.

"That's a pretty leg," quipped the boatman. "Too good to keep covered up like that."

Miss Pritchard blushed and her wrinkled, melancholy features looked young for a few brief moments. She snorted, half giggled and made her way to the middle of the boat, trying to recover her composure amidst the amused titters from the onlookers.

"Saucy fellow that," she confided in a whisper to Mrs Evans, who had now settled down beside her.

Finally the boat was full. We cast off, a procedure which intrigued me for there seemed endless lengths of rope tangled here and there, and headed off into the bay. There was a considerable swell and the small vessel almost stood on end one moment and disappeared into the depths of the sea as it entered a deep trough between the waves. I felt certain that I would never see the chapel or the farm again.

However, this initial fear soon passed and at least some of us began to enjoy the trip. Those who had taken seats in the front were already beginning to regret this, for, as the prow met a wave, a heavy spray came drenching down.

"Dieu, I'm getting soaked," yelled one not so enthusiastic passenger.

"Never mind, bach, you can't catch cold with sea water," consoled his companion.

What an experience this was! In my young imagination I was a merchant adventurer, braving the wide waters of the unknown, mastering the cruel elements to discover strange and exciting new lands. All we actually discovered was the coastline around Barry Island.

The rolling and pitching of the boat was having unpleasant effects on some of the passengers. Some had given up all pretence that this was an enjoyable experience and were hanging over the sides of the boat, regurgitating ham and salad to the benefit of the circling gulls.

Miss Pritchard had long since lost her temporary blush and had acquired a complexion resembling the surrounding water. She was gulping and swallowing hard.

"I wish I had never come on this old boat," she wailed. "I feel terrible. How much longer before we get back to dry land?"

A small child near her was busy eating a bar of chocolate, quite unconcerned by the queasy stomachs around him. Miss Pritchard's gaze alighted on him. She gave one heartfelt groan, abandoned her dignity and lurched to the side of the boat. There she stayed, a pathetic figure, until helped ashore at the end of the trip.

What fun this was! Here we were out on the wide sea with a sailor's view of the shore. How different everything looked from the other side of the coin — the coastline and the buildings and the gaily-coloured fairground in the distance. In the other direction there was nothing to be seen except sea and sky, and in the far distance the two merged. I wondered what we would see if we could go that far.

This was not to be, for the boat turned and headed back for the landing stage. The sick and the strong were finally disembarked. Home were the sailors, home from the sea!

The afternoon was flying past and soon it would be time to gather for tea before meeting the coaches for the homeward journey. This left us a short time to visit the fair. My brother and I had saved our pennies and had managed to collect a few shillings from benevolent aunts and uncles, and we were longing to go on the roundabouts.

"Now take care," said my mother. "Don't you dare go on the Figure Eight, it's much too dangerous. Besides, the thing might break down and then where would you be? Stuck up there all night."

We promised faithfully to stay away from the devilish contraption and scampered off lest she should change her mind. From the hall of mirrors we could hear shrieks of laughter, so we paid our money and went in. Young and old, fat and thin, tall and short were howling their heads off at the grotesque shapes of their reflections. In one corner there seemed to be even greater merriment and we made our way in that direction to find the cause of it.

The centre of attraction was Farmer, who was cutting a variety of capers in front of one of the mirrors. Even old John seemed to be losing some of his inhibitions, for the tears were streaming down his face, his head was thrown back and his mouth was wide open, showing his worn gappy yellow teeth as he roared his approval at Farmer's antics.

Farmer's self-importance was having a terrific boost now he was the centre of attraction, and the reactions of his audience spurred him on to even greater efforts.

"Har! Har! Har!" he roared. "Look 'ow wide I be," and his ginger beard filled the mirror like a great furze bush.

He swung round to face another mirror and became tall and thin except for his legs, which looked like two small stumps, while his beard now took on the appearance of a tall slim conifer.

"Look! Look! I be growed all of a sudden like." And he stood back to admire his new profile. He pulled faces and waved his arms to the continuing approval of the onlookers. With sides aching with laughter, we left to explore other parts of the fair. Hal and I took a ride in the ghost train, one which filled us with terror and made our hair stand on end.

On then to the roundabouts. We sat on separate horses which went sedately round and round and up and down, up and down to the accompaniment of the music from the organ. After an ineffectual throw at coconuts and a visit to the crazy cottage, we rejoined our family and friends for tea.

Aboard the coaches, we set off on our homeward journey, heads turned to look at the sea — our last for another year — until it was finally out of sight.

On the way out of Newport the coaches halted for ten minutes or so at a spot where the proverbial penny would be spent to prevent fidgeting on one's seat with legs crossed in desperation. There was also a fish and chip shop which did a roaring trade from the returning travellers.

The coaches were filled with the appetising smell of fish and chips and vinegar. The children wolfed theirs with great relish, whilst Miss Pritchard, who had now recovered from her distressing time on the boat, ate hers with great delicacy, one chip at a time held daintily between the tips of her forefinger and thumb.

There was a constant chatter concerning the events of the day. "That was a lovely old donkey I had a ride on. I wish my dad would buy me one."

At least I didn't have to worry about that. I could have a ride on our Neddy tomorrow if I wished to.

"Wasn't it a grand boat trip? Did you go on the boat?"

"We went on the ghost train — it wasn't half scary!"

"You should have seen Farmer Bailly and John Pryce in the hall of mirrors!"

"I'm sure that paddle did my corns good."

And so it went on.

The smaller children, after their exertions and excitement, were becoming drowsy. Small heads began to nod, eyes closed and they slept soundly until they were awakened at the chapel.

The dusk was gathering when we reached the farm. The rattle of the chain on the gate brought Sharp rushing out to meet us, his tail sweeping from side to side and his small, pearly white teeth bared in a simple friendly grin of welcome.

44

"Good dog, Sharp, you have guarded the farm for us," said my father, giving him an affectionate pat and a hug.

We entered the house and, whilst my mother busied herself getting us a nightcap of hot cocoa, my father set off to lock up the poultry for the night. The cows had been milked by a neighbouring farmer, so now we were all ready for bed.

Two sleepy little boys staggered up the stairs on legs almost too tired to support them. Soon we were back in the feather bed which we had left so early that morning with so much to look forward to, and now the sea was again so far away.

Our young bodies snuggled down in the feathers and the next instant we were fast asleep, to dream of all the wonderful events of the day.

CHAPTER
SIX

Christmas on the Farm

For Hal and me, December was a special month. Both our birthdays — Hal's was on Christmas Day — and, of course, Christmas itself, gave us ample cause for celebrations. But the great mystique of Christmas was the most exciting of all.

When we were children the seasons seemed to know their proper place in the order of things; summers were hot and dry and winters brought hard frosts and snow. December weather was Christmassy, with holly trees on fire with red berries and bunches of mistletoe hanging from the apple trees in the orchards.

The singing of carols at school and the party there led up to the excitement of Christmas. The great day of the year, when Father Christmas would come silently during the early hours and fill our stockings hanging at the foot of the bed, was getting nearer. There was much to be done on the farm as Christmas approached. For some weeks the young geese, cockerels, ducks and turkeys had been fed on a special diet to get them in prime condition for the festive table. The farmers' wives did a large trade in dressed poultry for the Christmas market. Each year this was held near Christmas Eve and was locally known as the "big market."

For a couple of days before "big market" the men killed the birds whilst the women with their helpers feathered and dressed them. Hal and I hated these days. There was goose down and feathers everywhere and one couldn't move inside or outside the house without becoming smothered by them. The down was used to fill the eiderdowns which covered our beds on cold winter nights, and the feathers to stuff the beds on which we lay.

The dressed poultry was tastefully decorated with sprigs of parsley or curly greens twisted through the folded wings or necks secured with skewers. Then they were laid out on slate slabs in the cold dairy, ready to be put into wrappings of grease-proof paper and then into big wicker baskets on "big market" morning.

How nice to have the house free of feathers again! However, there was little rest to be had. By three o'clock in the morning the grown-ups were already dressed and having an early breakfast, and by four o'clock, through the crisp frosty air, the sound of horses and traps on the Ross road could be heard and the great rush to be early at the "big market" was on. The farmers and their wives were muffled in their greatcoats against the biting wind and cold.

By the time I was five years of age the bus was beginning to provide an alternative means of transport. It was much quicker and more sheltered riding in a bus, even if it was jammed tight with passengers and baskets. On "big market" a special bus was laid on at an early hour.

One "big market" day sticks vividly in my mind. It was also Christmas Eve. My father had seen my mother off on the early bus and had then come back to the farm to carry on with the routine work of feeding the stock and milking the cows.

"Come on, boys, it's time you were up," he shouted from the foot of the stairs when he came in with the milk.

We were loath to leave our warm bed but the appetising smell of home-cured bacon set our nostrils twitching and our mouths watering.

"Up you get," said Hal, dragging the clothes off me and unceremoniously yanking me out of bed by my leg. Over breakfast my father told us of his plans for the day. He had rented some ground from a spinster lady so that he could increase the number of his stock. This ground was not far from the Grieg Hill and near my first school.

"I have to go and check the cattle at the Greig this morning," he said. "I think you had better come with me since I don't like the idea of leaving you here alone." On any other day this would have brought looks of dismay and strong protests. We went in that direction each day to school and we didn't want to be reminded of that.

But we were excited. The long-awaited Santa would soon be here and we understood that he had no presents for naughty children.

"Yes, we'll come," we said eagerly.

When breakfast was finished we put on our boots and warm coats and set off on our way. The journey didn't seem all that bad as we chattered excitedly about Christmas. My father, too, had caught the spirit of it and we were indeed a happy trio.

The cattle counted, we started on our way home. The bright frosty morning had become duller and above us the heavy sky let loose the first few flakes of snow. My father looked up anxiously. "I hope it doesn't snow much before your mother gets back," he said.

We were too young to understand his anxiety, too young to realise that heavy snow before evening might prevent our mother getting home in the bus. The first few flakes were followed by more and soon it was snowing heavily. To make matters worse, a wind had sprung up, so that by the time we reached home the ground, hard with frost, was white and drifts were beginning to form.

Hal and I stayed indoors for the rest of the day until evening, watching the snow get deeper by the hour. Just before dusk the storm ceased and we went out into the yard where the snow lay "deep and crisp and even".

"I know what we'll do," said Hal excitedly. "We'll make a landing place for Santa and his reindeer. Come on, get a shovel."

Armed with shovels we set to work. We battered the snow down hard in a corner of the yard and carefully smoothed it over. We stood back to admire our handiwork and called to our father to come and see what we had done.

"What is it for?" he asked innocently.

"It's a landing place for Father Christmas," I replied. "Do you think he'll use it?" I asked anxiously.

"I wouldn't be a bit surprised," said my father. "I'm sure he'll appreciate the trouble you've taken to help him."

It was now dark and the oil-lamp shed its welcoming glow through the living-room window. As time wore on, my father became increasingly worried and kept going outside to see if he could see the lights of the bus on the main road. Tea time had come and gone. The bus was nearly two hours overdue and we were all now very anxious.

What had happened? Had the bus been caught in a drift? Had it skidded off the road? All sorts of possibilities presented themselves to our minds and each one increased our anxiety. Then for the umpteenth time my father went outside to look. This time he came dashing back, relief showing on his face.

"It's coming at last," he said. "I'm going down to the road to meet your mother."

When my mother came into the house she looked worn out after her long day and the harrowing journey home. Both she and my father looked worried. "I can't think what has happened to it," she said. "I'm sure it was put on the bus. I saw the conductor put them all on before I got on the bus myself."

"But it wasn't there now," said my father.

"What's the matter?" chorused Hal and I together.

"Don't ask questions and don't bother us now," said our mother.

"But what is the matter?" we persisted.

"Well, there's a basket missing and it has all the Christmas presents in it and the shopping," replied my father.

Our faces fell. Our presents were gone and with them the Christmas goodies as well.

"Now think carefully," said my father gently. "Where did the bus stop?"

"Well, it stopped at a number of places," replied my mother. "Wait a minute, when it stopped at the blacksmith's shop in Llanvetherine the driver took a lot of baskets off to find Mrs Richard's baskets as they were all piled on top of one another and hers was at the bottom. It might have been lost there."

"I'll saddle up Bright and make my way to Abergavenny and check each place, starting at the blacksmith's."

My father set off into the night while my mother had a long-awaited and much needed meal. We sat fidgeting by the roaring fire, waiting impatiently for my father's return. We were torn between wanting to know if the basket was found and wanting to get off to bed early so that Father Christmas wouldn't miss calling at our house.

After what seemed an eternity we heard muffled sounds in the snow. The door latch rattled and there stood my father with the bulging basket on his arm. We all heaved sighs of relief.

"Where did you find it?" we all shouted together.

"At the blacksmith's. Old Jim happened to go outside and saw it by the side of the road. It was lucky that he did because it was snowing again and would soon have been covered over. He took it into the house and dried it by the fire."

Hal and I sat quietly while our parents talked about the market, what the prices for poultry had been and what a good market it was.

"Can we go to bed now?" we asked.

"Yes, come along, you must be asleep before Santa comes this way."

Eagerly we went upstairs, but not to our own room on this particular night. Our bedroom hadn't a fireplace and chimney so we changed rooms with our parents. Their room had a chimney and Father Christmas always came down this way.

We hung our stockings at the foot of the bed. My mother waited until we had said our prayers, tucked us up and kissed us goodnight. Soon we were fast asleep, dreaming of reindeer galloping across the sky.

My brother was always awake first on Christmas morning. His scrabbling about at the foot of the bed awoke me from my slumbers. As I stirred he said in a loud whisper, "Come on, wake up. He's been."

This brought me wide awake and I joined in the fumbling in the dark, both of us ignoring the cold air of the early morning. I think that my parents must have been lying awake waiting for the commotion to start, for they soon appeared in the doorway with a lighted candle.

"So he found his way all right, did he?" asked my father.

"I wonder what he has brought this time," chipped in my mother excitedly.

The candlestick was set down on the chest-of-drawers and the treasures were examined by one and all. The harsh notes of a toy trumpet rent the stillness of the morning, whilst Hal was lying on his tummy trying to retrieve a clockwork steamroller from under the washstand.

"Now back into bed or you'll both catch colds," said our mother firmly. "And stay there until it gets light."

With that the candle was doused and we were left once again in the dark, each with a new toy clasped under the bedclothes.

After what seemed an age the daylight grew stronger through the curtains and I could hear my mother downstairs busily preparing the breakfast whilst my father was outside attending to the stock. Now that snow lay thick on the ground there was a lot of work to do in foddering the animals. Christmas or not, they needed attention.

Hal and I dressed, gazing fondly at the new possessions which dear, kind old Santa Claus had brought us. How on earth he managed to visit all the children in one night I couldn't imagine.

When we went downstairs the room was gay with the mistletoe and holly which had been stuck up over the pictures and over the high mantelpiece after we had gone to bed. During breakfast my father, talking about the heavy snowfall said, "Father Christmas used the landing stage you prepared for him."

"Did he? How do you know?"

"Well, it's all covered with the hoof marks of his reindeer," replied our father.

We hastily finished our breakfasts, put on our boots and rushed out to see for ourselves where the reindeer had been. There, sure enough, were the marks of cloven hooves in the snow. So he had known in some mysterious way that we did try to help him. It was not for some years that I realised that my father had driven a couple of the cows over our carefully prepared platform of snow to convince us that the reindeer had been there.

Later in the morning, when all the outside work had been completed and all could relax until evening, the main presents were exchanged. Meanwhile, the appetising smell of roasting turkey was beginning to fill the air. What a day of contentment this was! Apart, that is, from a few minor squabbles between my brother and me over the new toys.

Boxing Day was always reserved for a shoot. After essential jobs were done, neighbouring farmers gathered at the farm to shoot over one another's ground. The game was chiefly rabbits, but if a partridge, pheasant or snipe rose in front of the guns they were illegally added to the bag.

Around mid-day the party converged on the farmyard to have an outdoor, standing-up snack of Christmas fare and cider. Cider was the universal drink the whole year round and, as a child, I cannot recall having seen any other intoxicating drink in the house, except perhaps a bottle of ginger wine, which was drunk with hot water at bedtime.

The local police officer always joined in the shoot. He either thought my father to be a law-abiding citizen or he was too thoughtful to ask my father for his gun licence. If he had done so, he would have had the embarrassment of taking him to court, for my father had never had one.

On Boxing Day night the adults played cards and my father smoked a rare cigar from a box which he had received as a Christmas present. The lovely aroma of cigar smoke filled the room and was part of Christmas to me.

During one afternoon just after Christmas, some children from cottages in a nearby hamlet came carol singing. They were poor and not very well brought up and they seemed unsure of the words of the carol which they were trying to sing. Their voices had more gusto than feeling as they sang, "O Hell, O Hell, O Hell, O Hell . . ."

My grandmother, who was in the house, snorted in disgust, "Just hark at those young heathens. But can you wonder at it, I don't think they have ever seen the inside of a chapel."

Nevertheless they were given a few coppers — more, I think, to halt their impious rendering than as a thanksgiving for their entertainment.

As Hal and I grew older and the mystery of Father Christmas was shattered, this festive season never seemed the same as when we were small children. Even so, away from the commercialism of the town, Christmas in the peace of the country seemed closer to its true meaning.

CHAPTER
SEVEN

William

Outside the living-room was a stone-paved walled yard with a paling gate which led out to the main farmyard. This small yard served to keep the animals at a healthy distance from the house. It had stone stairs leading to a granary above the cider mill and also a stone stile which provided an exit to the orchard, which had, in addition to apple and pear trees, huge walnut trees which yielded sacks of nuts each autumn.

The large farmyard was bounded on one side by a pond and on two other sides by the barn, stables and cattle sheds. Outside the cattle sheds was a huge dung heap whose size grew in winter and rapidly diminished in springtime when it was "muck spreading" season. Three exits led from the main yard, one to the rickyard, one to the "field-below-the-house" and one to the drive to the main road.

One day I was in the small yard when I heard the sound of the gate to the drive being opened. On looking up I saw a figure bending over to fasten the gate. It straightened itself, turned and walked towards me. He was tall, almost as high as the mantelpiece in the kitchen, broad-shouldered, and he walked with a spring in his step despite his heavy hobnailed boots. With arms swinging he marched towards me, a military man this if ever there was one!

He wore a cloth cap and blue serge jacket and trousers, and around his neck an artificial silk muffler of a nondescript colouring. As he drew nearer I could see that he had a large walrus moustache.

We were frequently visited by tramps, often of an unsavoury type, begging for food and drink. Thus as a small child I viewed his approach with some fear. Yet I could sense that he was different for he walked with a purpose and not a shuffling, couldn't-care-less gait like the typical tramp.

He stopped at the small gate and, from his towering height, looked down at the small boy timidly standing before him. His grave grey eyes looked at me kindly and, with a smile, he spoke.

"Is your father in, sonny?"

"I think so," I almost whispered. "I'll go and find him."

I went into the house.

"Daddy, there's a big man outside who wants you."

"Who is he?"

"I don't know. He has a bundle on his back but I don't think he's a real tramp."

My father came out.

"Good day, boss," said the stranger. He was not of these parts for he didn't speak in the drawling country accent of rural Monmouthshire.

"How do you do," replied my father. "And what do you want?"

The reply came in the concise, clipped tones of the stranger.

"I'm wondering if you could do with some casual labour for a while."

"Well, I'll have to think about it. Wait here a minute," and my father went into the house to confer with my mother, who had been observing the new arrival through the window.

Meanwhile I had been having a timid conversation with the stranger and was beginning to accept him when my father reappeared.

"What can you do?" he asked.

"Anything you want, boss. I can muck out the sheds, mend gates, make fowl houses, or any odd job you want done. All I ask is ten bob a week, my keep and a shakedown in the barn."

"All right, I'll give you a try-out for a few days."

"Thank you, boss — you won't regret it."

"What is your name?"

"Just call me William," he said.

And so William, as he was known to us, entered our lives for the first time. It was not to be the last either, and little did we realise then what it would mean to us in years to come.

William was as good as his word when it came to doing jobs about the farm. He was no milkman or ostler but he was an expert carpenter and joiner and could build almost anything he was asked to.

He had made a cosy bed for himself in the barn from clean sacks and hay. This he kept tidy, making it carefully each day. He came into the house for his meals and had a small table separate from the family. On winter nights, after the evening meal, he used to sit by the blazing kitchen fire smoking his pipe, stoked with dark shag, reading the newspaper, or at least he would read the paper when I wasn't chatting to him.

I had formed quite an attachment for William in a short space of time and we were now close companions. William could do almost everything, in my eyes. He could certainly play the tin whistle well and also the mouth organ. He told me that, when he was a young man at home, he played the cornet in a brass band.

"Why don't you play it now?" I asked.

"I haven't got one now, sonny. I pawned it one day and I haven't been back to reclaim it."

On most things he was forthcoming and informative but when I asked him about his home life, what his real name was and who and where his family were, he closed up and quickly changed the subject.

From his manners, his cleanliness and general behaviour we concluded that he had had a good family background, but just what it was remained a mystery for some years.

Every Sunday morning, winter and summer, when he was with us, William came to the house for a bucket of boiling water to carry out his routine of strip wash, shave and shirt washing. The washing was hung out to dry on a length of string in the rickyard and brought into the kitchen in the evening to air in front of the fire. The items of clothing were then carefully folded and the creases smoothed out by palming with the hands.

60

This meticulous attention to hygiene and tidiness was one of the facets to his many-sided character.

On the occasion of his first stay he had been with us some ten weeks and during this period he had rarely left the farm except to make an occasional excursion to Abergavenny on a Saturday afternoon to do some shopping.

Then without any warning it happened! He disappeared one evening and the only indication of his return was the barking of the dogs late at night when we were all in bed.

The next morning it was a morose William who, eyes red-rimmed and looking unkempt, came in for breakfast. He smelt strongly of drink and picked at his food. About mid-morning he disappeared again and was not seen any more that day. In fact for the next few days he was hardly seen at all and the only signs of his presence were the barking of the dogs at night and the empty wine and beer bottles strewn around his now untidy bed.

I was heartbroken that my friend had gone the way of a drunkard and was now becoming a social outcast.

"He'll have to go," said my parents. "He's in a disgusting state."

And so at the first opportunity my father told him to gather his belongings and clear off. William had saved his weekly earnings for one almighty blinder and had blown the lot. He set off on his lonely way, penniless, to his next port of call.

We were not wrong about his past in one respect. He was a veteran of the war and had served in the trenches in the thick of the fighting. If he had had a weakness for drink, then this experience, in all probability, had enhanced it.

However, perhaps a year later, William turned up again, very penitent, and asked for a job again. He was so useful and such a likeable chap that all was forgiven and he was soon busying himself with his crafts of carpentry and "improvising", as he used to say. He was also given jobs to do on the farms run by my grandfather and my uncles.

His stay at these farms invariably ended, as it did with us, with a bout of heavy drinking followed by the "boot".

Life on the farm went on as usual. Season followed season, crops were sown and harvested, stock was born, reared, fattened and sent for slaughter, and for months on end William would be forgotten except when we were reminded of him by his handicraft, which was evident around the farm.

In 1927 we moved to our new farm in South Monmouthshire and we never expected to see William again. But William's territory was far-reaching. He was a marathon walker. We knew that he roamed throughout the Forest of Dean, for he had often spoken of Cinderford and the surrounding area, and down the river Severn as far as Chepstow, but we had never heard him speak of the Pontypool district.

The new farmhouse and outbuildings were situated at the foot of a steep hill. One summer evening I was in the yard with my father when we glanced up the road which ran by the farm and then we saw him. There could be no mistaking the tall, familiar figure marching down the road towards us. William had found us again. We waited for him to draw near.

"Good evening, boss, hello sonny," came the crisp, cultured voice.

"Hello, William," we replied in unison. "How did you find us?"

"Well, I called at your old place and they told me that you had moved, so I made a few enquiries and here I am. Have you got a few odd jobs that need doing, boss?"

There was no denying that there was plenty for William to do, so despite the fact that there were now two pubs within easy walking distance and the temptation to go on a binge was even greater, William was taken on once again.

This time he took up his quarters in the narrow range of the cowshed and made himself his usual cosy bed of hay and clean sacks. By now I was around eleven years of age and spent much of my free time talking to him. He had travelled much and was something of a new dimension in my rather narrow way of life. He still played the tin whistle and the piccolo and we discussed music at length. He related stories of his life in France, in the trenches and in the lines. Only once did he mention having anything to do with a woman and then only briefly.

Many old servicemen returned home tattooed almost from head to foot. But not William, for his skin was unmarked.

★ ★ ★

One day he had taken one of our cows to be served by the bull of a neighbouring farmer. Artificial insemination hadn't been thought of then, or if it had, it certainly wasn't practised. Farmers didn't go to the trouble of keeping a bull unless the herd was very big, so the cows were taken to the bull.

On this occasion the cow had been served and was then tied up in the cowshed for a few hours. I happened to walk into the shed without William hearing me. He was talking to the cow.

"Well, old girl," he said, "I expect you feel better now that you've got some oil in your bottle."

And then he noticed me and, for the only time I can remember, he lost his composure and, believe it or not, actually blushed.

"Hello!" he said. "I didn't hear you come in," and he quickly changed the subject.

A few years later I had a Welsh collie bitch who had developed a liking for sucking eggs and it became necessary to keep her chained up during the day until the eggs had been collected. She was chained at the entrance to the open-ended implement shed in the rickyard.

One sunny summer morning a young heifer had just given birth to her first calf and William and my father were bringing mother and offspring from the field to the cowshed. Nip, the collie, rushed out, barking furiously as they passed the implement shed. Pandemonium broke out. The heifer, already in a state of tension and fearing for the safety of her calf, went berserk. She charged my father and tossed him into the air so high that, as he later remarked, he was looking down on the top of the rick of fern which had been gathered for bedding down the animals in winter.

He landed heavily, the breath knocked out of him. As he lay helpless on the ground, the heifer charged again with her long pointed horns, straight at my father. It was at that instant that William showed his true colours. Without a moment's hesitation he leapt forward, grasped the heifer by those dangerous horns and, with a superhuman effort, threw her on her side and held her down until my father could crawl to safety.

All William's previous drunken indiscretions were absolved by this one courageous act. We now owed him a great debt, which we could never repay. William, however, made little of the episode and showed great modesty about the whole affair.

As luck would have it, my uncle was visiting us for the day, so he promptly took my father into Abergavenny so the flesh would caused by the cow's horn could be properly dressed. The family doctor pronounced that he had had a very narrow escape and was lucky not to be more seriously injured.

The usual pattern of events followed. William eventually became restless, then hit the bottle and finally departed. We now felt sorry for him; sorry that he was afflicted in this way. He, too, felt that he disgraced himself by this behaviour and left of his own volition.

The periods between his visits varied. Sometimes it would be a few months and sometimes a year, but whenever he turned up a job was found for him. During one winter stay when I was preparing myself for the local scholarship examination he spent many hours with me in the evenings, wrestling over arithmetical problems.

Over the years a loose kind of understanding had grown up between us and I ventured to broach the subject of his family once again. After some hesitation he became more confiding.

"I have a married sister in Portsmouth and another in Pembroke," he said.

"Well, why don't you write to them? They must often wonder what has happened to you," I replied.

"Do you think I ought to?" he queried doubtfully.

"I'm sure you should. I know if I were in their shoes I would be always asking myself where you were or even wondering if you were still alive. Why not drop them a line?" I implored.

To my surprise, one Sunday evening he asked for a pen and paper and in a neat hand he proceeded to write to his sister in Portsmouth. By return of post came a letter addressed to Mr Rufus Morris, c/o our address. So William was really Rufus Morris but we continued to call him William.

The pleasure on his face was something to see when my father handed him the letter. He stroked his walrus moustache as he read it and, judging from his expression, the contents were pleasing to him. This was probably the first letter he had been sent in many years, and to receive one now from a sister who was dear to him must have given him great pleasure.

"She was so pleased to get my letter that she broke down and cried," he said. "She is going to Pembrokeshire with my brother-in-law to visit my other sister and would like to call and see me on the way — will that be all right with you, boss?"

"Of course, William," said my father. "Just you write and tell her to call."

One afternoon the following week a beautiful big saloon car drew up outside the farm gate where I was standing. Its occupants were an elegantly dressed woman of about sixty years of age and an equally elegantly dressed, handsome man of about the same age.

"Can you tell me, young man, if this is Wern Farm, the home of Mr and Mrs Thomas?"

"Yes," I replied. "This is it."

Then the woman spoke, rather hurriedly and excitedly.

"We are looking for my brother, Rufus Morris."

Trying to conceal the amazement I was feeling at such opulence and also the excitement of meeting William's relatives, who were so obviously well-to-do, I answered as calmly as I could but the words came tumbling out.

"William — um, Rufus — um, Mr Morris is expecting you. I'm so glad you've come. I'll open the gate for you — do drive in."

I opened the gate and the sleek black monster of a car glided into the yard. My mother came out to greet the visitors.

"Do come into the house — I'm sure you would like a cup of tea after your long journey," she said.

Meanwhile I had rushed off to find my father and William. The reunion was touching so we didn't linger and left them alone. When we rejoined them later, we found three radiantly happy faces. It was arranged that William's sister and her husband should spend the night with us before setting off for Pembrokeshire next day. That evening the three of them went for a walk and a chat before supper. No doubt they had a lot to talk about.

That night, after William had gone to bed in his own quarters, a situation which was rather embarrassing to all parties but one which had no ready solution, we had a long talk with his sister and brother-in-law, who was now retired but had been harbour master of one of the country's largest dockyards for many years. From a young man, William had been a rather wild and headstrong individual. Despite his good family upbringing he had acquired a liking for drink and, although his family had tried to dissuade him and get him back on to the right road, they had fought a losing battle. After the war they had rarely, if ever, heard from him.

The next day the visitors set off for Pembrokeshire, after arrangements had been made for them to break their homeward journey with us and, of course, William.

William's sister offered him a home with them and wanted to take him there when they returned. William, however, would have none of this, making the excuse that it would be difficult for him to sleep in a proper bed after all the years of living rough.

My parents and his sister exchanged periodic letters, and cards at Christmas. The following year when William was again with us he wrote to his sister, and arrangements were made for them to meet again at our home.

On this occasion, however, the visit was a disaster. A couple of days before his sister was due to arrive William started one of his binges. We wondered what would happen now. Would he control the urge, at least as long as his sister was present? Unfortunately this was not to be. William absolutely refused to see her and took refuge, and perhaps solace, in the pub.

His sister was broken-hearted by this turn of events and after waiting in vain for a couple of days in the hope of seeing him, she and her husband left for home. We never saw them again, although we kept in touch by letter.

During my late teens, after I had left the farm, I was home for a weekend, catching up with the local news, when my mother said, "I suppose you haven't heard about poor old William?"

"No! What's happened to him?" I asked.

"Well, he was working at Great House Farm when he became very ill, and Mr James went to see your uncle to find out what to do about him." My uncle was farming the adjoining farm and had employed William on numerous occasions.

"Well," continued my mother, "he was taken to Abergavenny hospital in an ambulance and was found to be suffering from pneumonia and chest complications. We wrote to his sister and told her what had happened so, as soon as he could be moved, she arranged for an ambulance to take him to Portsmouth."

"And how is he now?" I asked.

"In the last letter we had from his sister she said that he was making good progress and had promised that he would make his home with her and give up his wandering."

We were delighted with this news and felt that we had repaid, in a small way, the debt we owed him. However, our joy was short-lived, for a couple of weeks later we received another letter to say that Rufus, alias William, had had a relapse and had died a few days later.

We were greatly saddened by this news and felt that we had lost an old friend to whom we owed much. When the final reconciliation between him and his family had been achieved, it seemed so tragic that he had not lived for them to enjoy it.

CHAPTER
EIGHT

Haytime and Harvest

After the March winds and April showers came May and blossom time. The orchards were resplendent and the hedgerows were adorned with the white maytree flowers. The gay blooms of the ragged robin, wild parsnip and "hen and chicken" clothed the banks of the hedgerows and the meadows which were being kept up for hay.

The worker bees were busy in their thousands, buzzing from flower to flower and then, heavily laden, back to the hive with their precious loads. By their industrious labours they provided for themselves and humans, effecting the cross-pollination that was so necessary to induce the blossom to set into fruit.

High above the meadow a skylark soared free to the world, whilst not far away a more sinister bird of prey hovered in the sky. The hawk was looking for a tasty morsel. Suddenly he dived and then rose swiftly with his unfortunate victim.

As May faded into June the warm sun and steady showers made the hay crops grow rapidly. This was a busy time on the farm for, apart from the routine work which had to be done all the year round, there were the root crops to plant and to be kept free of weeds with the hoe.

With the grasses beginning to ripen and the June weather set fair, it was time to get the hay-making machinery out of the sheds where it had been stored since the previous haytime was finished. This to me was an exciting time. Variety was the spice of life!

All the equipment was horse-drawn. The mowing machine was fitted with a long pole and was drawn by a team of horses harnessed one on either side of the pole.

The first job was to give the machines a thorough oiling and greasing after their long period of idleness. Out in the rickyard my father was poking about with a nail to clear the oil-holes of grass-seeds and general dirt which would prevent the flow of oil to the working parts.

As a five-year-old I was following him around the machine with a large oil can, thoroughly enjoying myself, squirting the oil into the holes which he had cleared of dirt.

"Be sure you don't miss any," he said. "It's most important to oil everything well."

"This is a man's job," I said to myself. "No kid's stuff this, and much better than anything so childish as playing with a whip and top."

Having deluged one oil-hole I asked for his approval. "Is this all right?" I cried.

He came over to inspect my work and gave me an encouraging pat and replied, "That's fine — you're being a great help," a remark which made me stand full height.

The next job was to sharpen the triangular blades of the long machine knives. By now evening was drawing on.

"It's time you and Hal were in bed, so come along," said our father.

We went into the house, where Hal and I sat down to a light supper before going off to bed. It was so tiresome going to bed on light summer evenings when there was so much going on outside. But we knew that, as haymaking got into full swing, everyone would be so busy that our bedtime would get later and later.

My father went over to the barometer and tapped it.

"It seems set on fair," he said, "so I'll start mowing the top meadow tomorrow morning."

As the next day was Saturday this was exciting news, for we would be able to follow the machine and watch the quivering grasses fall to the clattering knives and then be swept into a neat swathe for the sun to turn it into sweet-smelling hay. We didn't know then that there would be sadness and despondency in the household the following evening.

Saturday morning dawned bright and sunny and we sprang from our beds without any urging. Outside the birds were whistling their merry trills. The air was already beginning to warm up as the sun poured from a cloudless sky. The green of the trees silhouetted against the beautiful blue inspired in me a sense of beauty. Up there, so I was told in Sunday school, was God in his heaven and all seemed right with our world.

My father had already got the two horses in from the field, and had given them feed to be getting on with in the stable whilst we had our breakfast. They were Jessie and her daughter Bright. Jess was docile and affectionate and, being the first mare my father had when he started farming, was a pet as well as a worker. Bright, however, was a skittish young girl and needed carefully handling at times.

"Well, I must be getting along," said my father, pushing his chair from the table and going out into the yard.

The clinking of chains from the stable told us that the horses were being harnessed with bridle, collar, hames and traces. We hastily polished off the remainder of our breakfasts and went out to join him as he led the horses from the stable. It was a matter of minutes to harness the team to the mower and then we were rattling off to the top meadow.

Hal and I ran ahead to open and close the gates between the fields. The knife guide was lowered to the ground, the knives fitted, a final check with the oil can and my father was on his way, cutting the first swathe. Hal and I followed behind the mower, fascinated by the toppling grass.

Sharp, the Welsh collie, trotted along beside us. Suddenly his keen eyes spotted something and he darted to one side. We followed him and saw a tiny brown shape wriggling through the grass.

"Look! Look!" we shouted. "A field mouse."

The tiny brown body couldn't outpace Sharp, who caught up with it, gave it a gentle nudge with his nose and then, having satisfied his curiosity, returned to follow the mower. After several circuits of the field our legs began to tire, so we sat the next one out and talked idly about things that small boys talk about and in a detached sort of way watched the team and mower make their way around the field.

"Whoa," shouted my father as the next round was completed. He got down from his seat, took off his hat and wiped his forehead.

"By golly, it's getting warm," he remarked and then, surveying the mowing with a critical eye, "Not a bad crop, is it?"

Then out with the oil can whilst the horses, now beginning to lather, had a brief respite. We boys went round to their heads and began feeding them with the sweet fresh grass. They flung their heads up and down and from side to disturb the flies which kept settling on their ears.

On Saturday afternoons my brother went to Abergavenny to have music lessons. Turning to us, my father said, "I think you had better go and get yourself ready. You don't want to miss the bus. Tell mother I will be down to lunch in about an hour."

Hal said, "Come on, we had better go." We returned to the house. Hal put on his best clothes, had an early lunch and went off to meet the bus.

My mother and I were waiting for my father to come to lunch and were listening for the clip-clop of horses' hooves to tell us that he was on his way. When he did come he was alone. One look at his ashen face told us that there was something very wrong.

"Whatever is the matter?" blurted out my mother.

"It's ... it's Jess," said my father in a scarcely audible voice.

"Well, what is it? For heaven's sake say," insisted my mother.

"She's broken her leg."

"Oh no! Are you sure? How did it happen?"

"She put her foot in a rabbit hole."

There was silence for a few moments while the awful truth sank in. I didn't realise, at my age, the full implication of what this meant. There was nothing that could be done to mend a horse's broken leg. Not only was Jess a valuable worker, but she was also a true and faithful friend.

"I'll go and fetch Davy Lewis to come and have a look at her," said my father, and immediately set off across the fields to the next farm to get another opinion.

"Can I go and have a look at her?" I asked my mother.

"No, you stay here with me," she replied, putting her arm gently around my small shoulders.

In what seemed next to no time my father was back with Davy Lewis, who confirmed that Jess's leg was broken. Somehow they managed to get her down to the rickyard. I wasn't allowed to go near. I think my parents wanted to spare my young feelings and didn't want me to see the poor animal suffering pain.

"What do you think I ought to do, Davy?" asked my father.

"Well, I don't think there's much that can be done," answered Davy. "I reckon you'll have to have her put down. It might be worth getting the vet out on the off-chance that he might be able to do something, but I don't hold out much hope."

"If we have to, will you do it?" pleaded my father. "I can't bring myself to shoot her," he continued, almost in tears.

"All right," said Davy. "But get the vet first."

My father set off on his bicycle to Cross Ash post office to telephone. Later that afternoon the vet arrived, took a look at Jess and confirmed our worst fears that there was nothing to be done.

"You'll have to have her put down," he said sympathetically.

I went into the field overlooking the Ross road and stood watching for the bus which would bring my brother back from his music lesson. Presently it came into sight and I ran down the road to tell him the sad news.

Around tea-time Davy Lewis returned. He went out of the house with the twelve-bore shotgun and turned into the rickyard. There was a loud report and it was all over.

During the evening Davy's two sons and daughters came up to play with Hal and me. We didn't play much. Somehow we found our way with dragging steps to the rickyard. There was Jess stretched lifeless on the ground with a gaping gunshot wound in her head. The end was merciful and sudden. The beautiful, gentle chestnut was no more. The day which had started so bright and

77

beautiful was drawing to its tragic close and we went to bed with heavy hearts.

In order that the hay-making was not held up, Davy lent us one of his horses whilst one of the colts was being broken in.

Bright now had to take her place between the shafts of the big wagon. She didn't take kindly to this, and when she was in one of her temperamental moods she nearly brought disaster on herself and the man who was loading the wagon.

The hay was being carted from a field with a steep bank, ending abruptly at the dingle through which ran the trout stream. With a full load, Bright was being urged on up the field. Suddenly she decided she had had enough for one day and she jibbed. The loaded wagon started to roll backwards and was poised on the edge of the dingle.

"Gee up, gee up, you bounder," yelled my father and the other men, in a frenzy. To lend weight to his words, my father gave her a whack across her rump with a pike handle. Bright promptly changed her mind and, with her belly almost touching the ground, started to pull in earnest. In the nick of time the danger was averted, or we must surely have lost another horse and the wagon to boot, to say nothing of the man on the top of the load.

In the sparsely populated countryside the air was clean and fresh, unspoilt by the grime and soot of industry and free of the acrid fumes of burnt sulphur spewed out from hundreds of town chimneys as they belched smoke from coal-fires.

The odours of the countryside came from the wild flowers, fresh vegetation, crushed leaves, manure and the natural but pleasant smell of healthy animals. And now the clean, sweet aroma of new-mown hay was added.

When it was considered to be sufficiently dry, the hay was raked up and piled into cocks — small heaps dotted about the fields. The neighbouring farmers always got together during haytime and harvest to help one another. Davy Lewis and my father always cooperated very closely and on Saturdays and in the warm evenings Hal and I either went to Davy Lewis's farm to play with his children or they came to us. It was great fun playing hide-and-seek amongst the haycocks, or rounders on the newly mown sward. After the wagon had been unloaded at the rickyard, it was filled with chattering, laughing children on the return journey to the hay-field.

During haytime, when the weather was settled, the men would work throughout the afternoon and evening until darkness fell, to get the hay into the barns or made into ricks before rain came. When the field was some distance from the house their tea was taken to them in large baskets and the hot tea itself in large enamel jugs.

Although large quantities of cider was drunk at this time, tea made a welcome change during late afternoon. It was most pleasant to sit in a shady corner of the field eating bread and cheese and young onions with home-baked cake to follow, on a hot summer afternoon, and then to laze for a few minutes, engaged in idle chatter or listening to the men's conversations.

"How be Jenkins Lower House getting on with his hay? He's always behind — never seems to 'ave things organised."

"No, 'e be a proper muddler. Not like Tom Jones of Pant — I hear he's about finished and soon starting on the corn."

"Is he now? I notice that field of winter wheat of his is ripening well."

"Aye, old Tom's got a good farm, everything in apple-pie order. Methodical is Tom."

And so the chat went on. Local gossip mostly. What else was there for them to talk about? At that time there was no wireless and no one bothered about taking a daily newspaper. News was chiefly passed from mouth to mouth and got enlarged and changed somewhat in the passing.

As I got older, games in the hay became a thing of the past and I found myself working alongside the men, doing a man's job and drinking my fair share of the cider. When I was in my teens I was out in the fields at four-thirty in the morning, mowing with a team of horses. At four o'clock it needed a lot of effort to drag myself from my bed. But once the effort had been made, what a joy it was to be out in the clean early morning air! We were then hard at it throughout the day, working on the hay which had been cut a couple of days previously, turning it, raking it into rows and then carting it to the rickyards. We were often bringing in the last load of the day late at night by the light of the clear moon. Horses and men were glad to snatch a few hours' rest before repeating the performance again the following day.

When I was studying for my matriculation I often took my books into the hay-field in the evening. There I was joined by Greta, who was also working for the same examination. This was all very pleasant in the hay but hardly the right conditions for learning Latin syntax.

One of the farmers who was helping in the field passed us by and gave me a knowing wink.

"I reckon you're more interested in that young lady's legs than them books," he said, giving a glance in the direction of Greta's very short gymslip. I pretended not to hear him but thought that he knew what he was talking about.

Making good hay requires good weather, and sound judgement on the part of the farmer. If it is left too long in the scorching sun, the quality is lowered, but if it is stacked too quickly when too green or damp, it heats to such an extent that it becomes mouldy and unpalatable to the animals and, in extreme cases, spontaneous combustion can occur.

In order to test whether a hay-rick was overheating, my father used a long iron rod, one end of which was shaped like half an arrowhead. The rod was pushed into the rick and left for a few minutes to attain the temperature of the hay. It was then dragged out, pulling a piece of hay with it. My father could judge the condition of the hay by the feel of the iron and the smell of the sample pulled out of the rick. If heating occurred to a dangerous degree, a hole was cut through the centre of the rick to allow the heat to escape.

On one occasion it was necessary to do this with some oats which we had stacked in the barn. I thought it might be rather funny to play a joke on some school friends who were visiting me. I placed a few light sticks across the hole and then gently laid some straw on the sticks.

"Let's go on the corn rick," I said to my friends.

They needed no second bidding and I led the way to the far side, carefully skirting the hole.

"Come on," I shouted. "Come over here."

One boy darted across and, with a loud yell, disappeared from view. I suppose the hole was about eight or ten feet deep. We hauled him out; he was rather scared by his experience.

Some days later I was going to repeat the performance with another friend and prepared the "animal trap" as before. In my eagerness to trap my victim I carelessly crossed the straw, forgetting where the hole was hidden. This time it was I who disappeared from view, much to the consternation of my companion, and with rather disastrous results to myself. On hitting the bottom I jack-knifed and caught my nose a resounding thump on my knee.

This was a case of the biter bitten!

I crouched dazed for a few moments in the blackness of the hole and then painfully started to clamber out.

Over the edge of the hole a face peered anxiously down at me. A galaxy of stars danced before my eyes and blood poured from my nose as, with the help of my friend, I staggered towards the house. My mother stood horrified at the sight of the casualty coming towards her.

"What on earth have you done?" she cried.

Explanations were rather garbled as she wiped away the blood with a cloth soaked in cold water but, when the truth of the episode dawned on her, her sympathy was short-lived.

"It serves you right for being so stupid. You might have killed someone with an idiotic trick like that."

I couldn't argue with these sentiments, for had I not experienced at first hand the milder consequences of this folly?

Over the next few days my nose, swollen to such an extent that it seemed to cover most of my face, assumed most of the colours of the rainbow. Never in all the time that I was boxing and playing rugby football did my nose receive such brutal treatment.

It was usually a rush to get the hay-making completed before the corn harvest was started. The cornfields had gradually been undergoing a change of colour as the ears of wheat, oats and bearded barley began to ripen.

Meanwhile, the binders had been undergoing an overhaul and were now standing ready to go into action. The corn needed to be just right for reaping because over-ripe corn shredded the grain too readily and much could be lost.

Hal and I followed the binder around the field for miles, watching the fan blades sweep the corn on to the knives. Then the canvas conveyors swept it up into the body of the reaper, compressed it into a tidy bundle, tied it and ejected a neat sheaf of corn on one side of the machine.

I remember, when I was a small boy, following the reaper when my uncle was riding it. Suddenly my cap was snatched from my head and thrown on to the corn on the canvas. I watched it being swept away into the reaper and thought that it had gone for ever.

"My . . . my cap's gone," I almost blubbered at my uncle, who was roaring with laughter, thinking this a huge joke. Then a sheaf popped out.

"Have a look in that sheaf," he shouted back. I fumbled about in the sheaf and there, sure enough, was the cap. After that I pestered him to do it again and again.

There was quite a lot of sport to be had when corn was being cut. The cornfields of Monmouthshire seemed to be full of rabbits. The reaper always started its work on the outer perimeter of the field and, as the cutting continued, the area of standing corn diminished. The rabbits, afraid of the noise, tended to migrate to the centre of the field to take cover in the uncut corn.

As the area grew smaller the tension and excitement grew greater. A small army of adults and children, armed with sticks and stones, stationed themselves at various places around the standing corn, waiting for the rabbits to break cover. Whenever one made a run for it the hubbub was terrific.

"Hi-yi-yi, there he goes," went up the chorus, and the chase was on. Dogs, barking furiously, joined in the chase after the rabbits, leaping over the sheaves lying on the ground. More got away than were caught by this technique.

Other times, men with guns were stationed around the field and on these occasions the bag was higher. On late August evenings, as dusk was beginning to fall, the shouts of the hunters could be heard above the clatter of the reapers from farms far and near on the other hillsides.

On more than one harvest, foxes were shot as they broke cover from the cornfields. The sheepdogs joined in the hunt and it was interesting to watch the skill of one of them. She walked around the outer perimeter of the field, watching the wall of standing corn alertly.

When a rabbit broke cover, she slid along the stubble almost on her belly until she was in the path of the approaching animal and then hid herself behind a sheaf. Then, at the critical moment, she popped up from behind the sheaf so that the rabbit literally stepped into her waiting jaws. This sport may, at first sight, appear cruel to the reader but rabbits did immense damage to crops and it was necessary to control their numbers. This was far less cruel than the introduction of myxomatosis in later years.

Likewise crows, jays and wild pigeons or quists, as they were called in Monmouthshire, damaged the corn crops when the sheaves were stacked in stooks in the fields. When I was old enough to carry a shotgun I used to spend an afternoon in the cornfields waiting for the marauders to appear.

One summer when I was staying at my grandfather's farm he said to me, "Those quists are playing havoc in the wheatfield. Go and see if you can shoot a few of them. I fancy a couple of roast quists for my dinner."

I took the double-barrelled twelve-bore and a pocketful of cartridges and made my way to the wheat-field. When I arrived there, a host of birds rose from the stooks and flew off to the tall trees lining the banks of the trout stream. I made a hide in the middle of the field and sat down to wait patiently, keeping quite still. At intervals I peeped through the sheaves to see if my quarry had returned.

Then they were there. Not more than thirty yards or so away, perched on top of a stook, were two pigeons, a crow and a jay, all feeding together. I took careful aim and squeezed the trigger. Bang! A cloud of birds rose in all directions but, seeing no movement, they soon settled again. Another shot and I went to see what I had got.

With the first shot I had bagged two pigeons, a crow and a jay, and with the second shot, another pigeon. The jay and crow were tied to sticks and set up in the field as a warning to other birds of the fate in store for them if they dared to venture back to steal more grain. I gathered up the three quists and set off for the house, thinking of the tasty meal in store for us.

After standing in the stooks for two or three weeks — depending on the weather — the sheaves were brought into the barns and rickyards to be stacked until the threshing machine came to the farm.

The threshing drum and the machine which gathered the threshed straw and tied it into bundles were towed from farm to farm by an enormous traction engine. This also provided the power to drive the machines while they were operating.

Threshing was an annual event; it was an entertainment for the youngsters and broke the monotony of the adults' day-to-day routine.

When one thinks of the inaccessibility of many of the farms, approached by rough mud tracks, one realises why a large traction engine was necessary to draw the heavy equipment. Before these monsters were developed, teams of horses were used, and often the machines were bogged down in mud on some remote farm for hours on end. The threshing machine could be late by hours or sometimes days arriving at the next farm.

The threshing drum was drawn into position alongside the stack and then the baler and engine were lined up with it at either end. This had to be done carefully so that the driving belts were not under strain and did not come off the driving wheels. At last all was ready, but it was too late in the day for threshing to commence.

The relative quiet of the autumnal morning was broken by the clang of the shovel as the engine driver started to get up steam. This noise awoke Hal and me and we realised through the fog of sleep that this was threshing day.

"Come on get up," shouted Hal, leaping out of bed and dragging all the clothes off me.

"Shut up," I replied peevishly and clawed at the bedclothes.

I have always had great difficulty in rousing myself in the morning and to get from the horizontal to the vertical required a supreme effort.

However, the stoker was doing his job well, for I could hear the hiss of steam coming from the yard where the engine stood. There would be no more rest now, so I dressed and went downstairs, where the family were just about to sit down to breakfast.

We had barely finished our meal when one or two farmers and their workers began to arrive from nearby farms to help out for the day. It was customary for farmers to help one another on special occasions such as this. I think they all enjoyed themselves and made it a social, gossipy gathering. It was the wives playing hostess for lunch and high tea who had the most arduous time, having to feed twelve or fourteen hungry men twice on one day.

Huge dishes of roast beef and boiled bacon, together with dishes of potatoes, parsnips and carrots were set upon the table, but at the end of the meal it looked as if a swarm of locusts had passed that way.

The work was soon under way and the constant hum of the drum changed to a more urgent note as each sheaf was thrown into it. A cloud of dust arose over the area; the threshed straw spewed out at one end and the grain at the other end. The grain poured from several different spouts, having been graded by screening according to size. Top quality grain filled the sacks on the left and tares the sacks on the right. Underneath the drum an ever increasing heap of chaff began to form.

It was hard work while it lasted and a very dusty job too. At last the harvest was complete. All was safely gathered in, "Ere the winter storms begin".

The harvest festivals could now take place and the farmers and their kind could give full fervour to "Here we come rejoicing, bringing in the sheaves".

CHAPTER
NINE

Chapels

The Nonconformists were strong in Wales and Monmouthshire and each Sunday would find them in full and fervent voice in the chapels in the towns and in the country parishes. The Wesleyans, Primitive Methodists, Baptists, Congregationalists and Presbyterians poured from their homes to their respective places of worship, clad in best Sunday clothes: the men sombre in black, the women in ankle-length wool or cotton dresses and coats with wide-brimmed hats often of elaborate floral design.

Each season of the year brought special occasions which called for feverish activity in preparing for them: harvest festivals in the autumn, carol services at Christmas and the eisteddfods and tea parties in the summer.

The local chapel which we attended as a family was a small stone-built building consisting of a porch, the larger room where the congregation sat, and a small vestry. A gravel path led from the main road through the graveyard to the front porch. Tombstones, some elaborate and some of plain stone, in varying states of maintenance, surrounded the chapel and told the world of the names and ages of previous worshippers now departed.

Stones covered with green lichen which obscured the details of the departed, and tall grass around, indicated the resting place of those whose families had become extinct, or had moved away or who no longer cared. Others, more elaborate in carved and polished marble, indicated the resting places of well-to-do farmers.

The stone building had no damp-course and became very dank in winter. In summer it was cool even in the hottest weather. The chapel was lit by a number of oil-lamps suspended from the ceiling. The odour of paraffin, damp walls and polish from the pine-wood pews blended together to give an unforgettable smell of chapel.

On winter nights my parents, brother and I trudged the mile and a half to the evening service. In the front pew sat the elders and the deacons, white-haired and white spade-bearded. The circular coke stove stood near the centre of the chapel and, when it was well stoked, radiated a constant current of hot air which offset to some extent the clawing dampness. The soft illumination from the oil-lamps gave a certain cosiness to the scene. Apart from the pews and the high pulpit, a pedal organ standing in front of the pulpit completed the general furnishings.

Most of the country chapels in the area were similar but those in the towns were much larger, more ornate, better maintained and were the proud possessors of a varnished pine-wood balcony on three sides of the chapel. At harvest festivals and eisteddfods they were packed to capacity, for congregations from neighbouring chapels made a point of going to one another's special functions.

As a small child I sat demurely in the pew with my brother. Our mother sat between us for, as the sermon wore on, we became restless and she was obliged to give us constant nudges and disapproving looks to keep us in order. We were told that it was very naughty to misbehave in chapel. My father was the organist and thus did not sit with us.

However, it appears that during the earlier days of Nonconformism the sermons sometimes lasted for three hours and the deacons used to patrol the aisles with long bean poles for prodding the nodding worshippers into wakefulness so that they might not miss any of the minister's words of wisdom.

The ministers of my childhood were most fervent in the delivery of their sermons; they also used a form of psychology in their approach, but might not have realised it. I well remember one preacher who, to get a point over, would prance around the pulpit like a caged lion, waving his arms and shouting at the top of his voice. The congregation would sit bolt upright, heeding every word and watching the performance with great interest, but, lest this torrential storm of words and frenzy should swamp the mind and exhaust the listener, the tempo would suddenly change and a great calm would settle.

The preacher's voice was now reduced to a whisper, the congregation leaning forward intently to catch his every word, then, suddenly, when it was becoming lulled into approaching somnolence, the hurricane burst forth again and the sudden blast swept the listeners back against their seats. No need of bean poles with this technique!

The attentive, white-bearded elders drank in every word. When the preacher made a point of which they approved, or perhaps understood, they were fervent and voluble in their approval.

"Amen to that!"

"Hear! Hear!"

"Allelujha!" cried the elders, nodding their heads and shaking their beards.

Such encouragement produced greater efforts from the preacher. This was team work if ever there was!

After the service everyone began to file out, spiritually refreshed to meet the rigours of the coming week.

The chapel was not only a meeting place for worship but also a centre where friends and neighbours from widely spaced farms and houses met once a week. The topics of conversation turned on the weather, the chances of a good crop or how the market was faring.

"Hello, Jack. The preacher was in good form tonight — good sermon, wasn't it?"

"Aye, you're right, Dan. You got your winter corn in yet?"

"Just about, but that bottom field of mine is very wet. I'm thinking I'll have to put some land drains in down there but it's so darned expensive."

"Aye, that's so, but 'ave you 'eard about poor old Bill Morgan from Penyclawdd Farm?"

"No, what's happened then?"

"Had to have his pigs destroyed — all got swine fever."

"Dieu! That's a loss for him, especially with the market picking up. They tell me pigs was fetching a price at Abergavenny market last week."

"Ah well! That's how farming goes — all ups and downs. Must be off now, it's getting a bit nippy. Looks like a frost tonight." Then turning to my brother and me, "Goodnight, young fellers."

My mother, who had been chatting to the other wives, rejoined us and without further delay we started off for home.

The night was dark but from the grassy banks by the hedgerow shone a luminescent light from glow-worms. Hal and I began collecting them in our caps, thinking that they would give us sufficient light to see our way home. It was quite extraordinary the amount of light which these small creatures emitted when gathered together en masse.

The Tea Party was usually held in June when hay-making was in full swing and the weather was warm and settled. My grandmother, who lived a few hundred yards above the chapel, made available her best china and silverware for the occasion.

My most vivid memories of these parties was the plentiful supply of rich cherry and seed cake. This was the one time of the year when I savoured the taste of caraway seeds. The cake was obtained from the bakery and was not home-made. Except for a small general stores about two miles from the farm, the shops of any consequence were about seven miles away in Abergavenny. However, apart from the inconvenience in shopping, we lived almost entirely on home-produced food. The staple foodstuffs such as butter, cheese, eggs, poultry, bacon and milk were all home-produced and it was considered a treat to have something which had been obtained from a shop.

There was much activity behind the scenes in preparing for this annual event and a considerable amount of rivalry and petty jealousy as to who would do what.

"I'll 'power' the tea," said Mrs Evans, sweeping aside all other claimants for this most important part of the proceedings.

"She'll pour the tea? Indeed she will not," said Mrs Price indignantly to her cronies. "I've always poured the tea — who does she think she is? Does she think she owns the chapel then?" her voice becoming shriller with every word.

However, on the day the personal enmities were all submerged beneath the surface and smiles and goodwill abounded. This was an occasion for the Sunday finery to be brought out. The ladies in their silk dresses with wide-brimmed hats looked resplendent; the children had their boots brightly polished. The men, now that summer had arrived, had discarded their breeches and leggings for drainpipe trouser suits, and Sunday black was replaced by suits of brown.

I think the party was arranged by the ladies for the ladies. Those of us children who were at school went straight to the party and, as this meant a walk of some two and a half miles, we didn't arrive until late in the afternoon. The menfolk were much later getting there as they were loath to leave the hay-fields when the weather was so good. By the time we arrived the ladies had done justice to the fare provided and, no doubt, over innumerable cups of tea, had indulged in the biggest gossip session of the year. However, a plentiful supply of cake had been kept by for the new influx of ravenous young mouths.

The younger children, who had been present all the afternoon, were now becoming rather tired and short-tempered. Little Dewi Griffiths had been quite a handful all the afternoon and seemed to delight in stuffing bits of sticky cake down Gwyneth Williams's neck, an act which made Gwyneth pipe her eye, messed up her party frock and brought looks fit to kill from Gwyneth's mother. He almost brought off the coup of the afternoon by dragging at the tablecloth.

"Dewi! Stop it at once," cried his mother. "You naughty boy — just wait until I get you home!"

"Wait till she gets him home, indeed," whispered Mrs Evans to her spinster friend, Miss Llewellyn. "Mark my words, she'll have trouble with him if she doesn't mind things."

Dewi was prevented in the nick of time from bringing my grandmother's best china crashing to the ground.

The womenfolk began to clear up the debris — cakecrumbs, the lone, trodden-on, squashed cherry and the tea-leaf-bespattered cups and saucers. Cloths were shaken and folded, left-over cake packed to be taken home by one or another, and all got down to the business of washing up.

Soon the menfolk arrived to collect their respective families. Dewi, now subdued, his eye-lids drooping, went home pick-a-back with his father, sucking his thumb.

All was still again, the summer evening air, the trees and the chapel with its silent sleepers.

A great occasion for the chapel was the annual eisteddfod. For weeks before the event took place, children and adults were learning their recitations and practising their solos from Handel's *Messiah*.

Sunday school lessons were given over to rehearsals and the adults got together in the evenings for choral practice. Sometimes there came visiting soloists from the hills and valleys; sopranos, contraltos, basses and tenors with voices clear as bells who showed the locals how it should really be done.

"Mind you, Elsie Pritchard do have a nice voice but she couldn't quite reach top C. She was quavering a bit on the top notes. But Miss Jones from the Rhondda, Dieu, she was magnificent. I never heard a voice like it!"

This was the only standard by which judgement could be made as the wireless was still a rarity in these parts.

The competitors sat in the front pews and the minister announced each one as their turn came to perform.

"And now, my friends, we are going to have a recitation from Gwyneth Williams entitled 'Twinkle, Twinkle Little Star'." In the hush of the little chapel, save for the creaking of a pew, a small four-year-old made her way to the platform. In a nervous, lisping sing-song voice she began.

> Twinkle, twinkle, little star,
> How I wonder where you are,
> Um . . .

A long pause. Head held low, handkerchief being twisted in her small hot hands, she stood silent and alone on the wide lonely platform.

A whispered word from the prompter got her going again and, as if to get the ordeal over and done with, the tempo increased until, at last, she was able to toddle from the platform, now beaming, flushed and relief written large on her small features.

And so it went on, the older children reciting in turn the "Glory of the Garden" to see who would be awarded the prize by the adjudicators. Similarly the adult choirs competed for the best rendering of the set choral piece.

The following week the *Abergavenny Chronicle* was eagerly read by the competitors, who liked to see their names in print.

★   ★   ★

The ministers were fond of using similes and metaphors to illustrate points in their sermons when Welsh oratory was given full vent. In the remoter country districts it was not always possible to get the services of a minister and at such times a lay preacher would fill the gap. Often he was a local farmer.

On one occasion at a very tiny chapel near the Greig Hill, Jack Edwards of Cefn Farm was taking the service. In the front pew sat another farmer, Price Thomas.

We must digress for a moment to explain the meaning of a local idiom. When pigs root in the fields and turn up the turf to search for grubs and plant roots, the term used to describe the tearing up of the turf by the pig's snout is "mooting" from the verb to "moot". To prevent damage to the pastures a ring is put in the pig's snout. This deters him or her from carrying out what, to the farmer, is this act of vandalism.

On this Sunday evening Jack Edwards, with great fervency, started his sermon thus.

"Oh, the Devil's like a big black pig and he'll moot you and moot you and moot you."

Immediately up jumped Price Thomas and, with eyes raised to the ceiling of the chapel, he piously intoned, "Ring him, dear Lord, ring him."

At another chapel the minister had finished the Sunday morning service and was in the vestry when he asked his deacon what the congregation thought of his sermon that morning.

"Well, they enjoyed the sermon very much," replied the deacon, "but you used one word which they didn't understand."

"Oh, indeed! And what word was that?"

"Phen-om-en-on."

"I must try and put that right," replied the minister.

At the Sunday evening service as he was about to commence the sermon he said, "I understand, my friends, that in my sermon this morning I used a word which you didn't comprehend. That word was phen-om-en-on. I will do my best to explain it to you.

"If you were walking down the road one day and you looked over a gate into a field and you saw in the field a cow, that would not be a phen-om-en-on. And if you walked on down the road and you stopped at another gate and you looked over the gate into the field, and you saw in the field a thistle, that would not be a phen-om-en-on. And if you walked further down the road and looked up into the sky and saw in the sky a skylark singing to high heaven that would not be a phen-om-en-on either. But if you walked on down the road and stopped at a gate and looked over the gate into the field and you saw in the field a cow sitting on a thistle singing to high heaven like a skylark, that would be a phen-om-en-on."

During the winter months a lecture would occasionally be given in the chapel with the aid of a magic lantern. At five years of age this contraption was, to me, magic indeed. The lantern was set at the back of the chapel and the pictures, highly coloured, appeared on the wall behind the pulpit. This early form of visual aid, crude by today's standards, brought to life the biblical stories in a way which I had not thought possible. I sat enthralled through the whole performance.

As these chapels were in agricultural areas the harvest festivals were well supported both in produce and in worshippers who filled the chapels to bursting point in their desire to give thanks to God, who had blessed their labours and the land to yield of its fertility in such abundance.

The chapels were decorated with autumn flowers and almost every indigenous vegetable and root crop was represented in profusion. The pulpit was almost obliterated with ears of corn, whilst sheaves of it stood around the chapel where space permitted. All the produce was sent to the cottage hospital in Abergavenny later in the week.

The chapel was filled to capacity. The oil-lamps shed their soft glow and the minister stood up to announce the first hymn. From the throats of people with thankful hearts came the notes of "We plough the fields and scatter the good seed on the ground". The sermon was good, the singing was good and all left at the end of the service with a feeling of well-being. God had fulfilled himself, and His people had given thanks that He had done so.

The Baptists still received members into their Church with the same fundamental rites as John the Baptist used on the banks of the Jordan. I remember the baptism of my maternal aunt when I was a small child.

A tank of water submerged below ground level substituted for the river Jordan. Mr Cule, the Baptist minister who lived with us, performed the ceremony. My aunt, in company with others who were about to undergo baptism, was clothed in a long white dress. One weekday afternoon, Mr Cule, standing up to his thighs in the water, took my aunt in his arms and lowered her into it. Together with the appropriate words, this constituted the ceremony of baptism.

My aunt, dripping with water, repaired hurriedly to the vestry to change into dry clothes and take a cup of hot tea. At yet another Baptist chapel at Pandy the ceremony is carried out more in keeping with the method employed by John. The river Honddu flows past the chapel yard. Steps lead down to the water and here the minister immerses the new member. The waters, coming from the mountains, are icy cold but, to my knowledge, no-one has even sneezed through being immersed. If they had dared to bathe in the river they would probably have contracted a severe chill. Who says there is no such thing as faith?

It was on some chapel function — I can't recall what — that I had my first ride in a motor car. To me it was just a motor car but, looking back, I think it was a Model T Ford or something very similar. It was about the only car in the district and was referred to by all the locals as Dai Evans's tin lizzie.

It was very exciting to be taken out one winter night to drive to Abergavenny. The trip was somewhat marred by the fact that my brother and I sat in the back seat

102

with Dai Evans's son, who was rather spiteful and tormented me for most of the way. Perhaps he resented my sharing his father's new car with him. I seem to remember that it was a wet and windy night, for the canvas hood on its strong wooden supports flapped and fluttered in the wind. It seemed that we travelled at enormous speed but we probably never exceeded twenty-five miles an hour.

My parents and grandparents had been brought up with strict Victorian rectitude and Sunday was a day of rest in the strictest sense. Only essential work was done on Sunday and music of a secular nature was forbidden. No fun and games on Sunday!

I, being rather high-spirited, found this somewhat irksome at the time and regular chapel-going was something to be endured. However, it instilled into me the difference between right and wrong and, although I didn't understand the scriptures as I might have done, it gave me a moral fibre which was to guide my actions in later years.

CHAPTER
TEN

Grandfather's Farm

It was always with great excitement that I went to stay on my grandparents' farm. It was much bigger than ours; there was always more happening on a bigger scale and I suspect that I was thoroughly spoilt by my grandparents and my mother's sister, who was a young woman in her early twenties when I was a toddler.

It was situated some three miles from my first home and, for the greater part of the distance after leaving the main road, the journey was made over a narrow, twisting road with deep ruts in places on either side. The trap would lurch and heave, jolt and rattle until one felt that every bone in one's body would be dislocated.

Often my grandmother fetched me with her pony and trap and, even as a small child, she left me in no doubt as to what she thought of the local rural district council officials who allowed the roads to get in such a state.

"It's disgraceful the way they neglect these roads. They ought to be made to use them themselves, then we would have something done," she said.

I agreed that "they", whoever "they" were, were a thoroughly bad lot, and such a sympathetic understanding of this problem put me in rather a good light with my grandmother. Jolting apart, the drive was always a pleasant one for, in between the frequent outbursts about the state of the road, we would chat cosily about nothing in particular.

"Farmer so-and-so has got a good crop of wheat this year, and don't that herd of Herefords look in good fettle?"

I nodded agreement for I was not old enough to judge whether the Herefords were in good fettle or not. Meanwhile Kitty, the pony, plodded her steady way up the steep hill until she reached the top of the rise and then, with a flick of the reins, she would get into a steady trot, glad to be on her homeward journey. We went down the hill into the next small valley, past a few cottages known as the Bont, and up the hill on the other side.

There was one particular house we passed which never failed to evoke a torrent of caustic remarks from my grandmother. In some ways she was a haughty woman but she was also gentle and kind. Her Victorian upbringing made her have little time for fast-moving modern ideas, whilst sluts and slovens got little shrift from her.

It was customary in those days for farmers and some cottagers to fatten a pig for bacon, which was salted down to provide, apart from the fresh pig-meat and offal, bacon and ham for the rest of the year. It appeared that this particular cottager killed a pig and butchered it on the side of the road and was too indolent to remove the entrails from the roadside. The stench from the decomposing remains was soon apparent and my disgusted grandmother voiced her opinion of the fellow in no uncertain terms whenever we passed the house.

"Did you ever hear of such a thing? Have you ever heard of anything so disgusting? The brute should be summoned. Why nobody did anything about it I shall never know," she said. Whenever I pass that house now, I always think of the pig which was slaughtered on the side of the road.

Eventually we reached the public house where beer was drawn from the wood and rough cider was drunk in large quantities by the farm labourers, who found it tasty and cheap.

"A proper den of iniquity that place," said my grandmother as we turned right into an even more deeply rutted road. "They're a lot of drunken sots that get in there — the place should be closed down. Those Randall brothers go there and drink themselves silly and then fight in a fearful way. Only last week two brothers set about the other — on his birthday, mind! — and blacked his eye, and his nose was spurting blood like a fountain."

My childish mind conjured up the ghastly scene and I shuddered at the evil influence of the potent liquid. However, this didn't stop me toddling to the cellar with my grandfather and having a sip of his cider.

By now the road was running alongside the farm fields and soon the grey stone buildings of the huge barns hove into sight. As we passed the barn a row of grinning foxes' skulls, nailed high above the massive barn doors, looked down on us. These were victims of the Monmouthshire Hunt, previous raiders of the poultry houses who had paid the ultimate penalty for daring to indulge their taste for fowl flesh.

As we passed the barn the big stone house came into view. The barren greyness of the stonework was broken by the mass of Virginia creeper which covered the walls, whilst the porch was enveloped with the clinging foliage of Japanese honeysuckle.

In front of the house was a well-kept lawn and this was separated from the quadrangle-shaped farmyard, which stood at a lower level, by a stone wall. On one side of the house was a walled kitchen garden which trapped the sun and was my grandfather's pride and joy. On the other side of the house was a large orchard where, apart from apple, pear and plum trees, there grew many large cherry trees which provided an abundance of golden cherries, much to the enjoyment of birds and humans alike.

Kitty's clip-clop brought the farmhand hastening to the gate.

"Hello, young fella, and 'ow be you, then? Come to stay with Gran then, 'av you?"

"Very well, thank you. Yes," I replied.

We got down from the trap and went into the house through the front door. The hall was large and dark. To the left was a very big dining room which contained a long polished mahogany table, rounded at both ends. On Sundays there would be family gatherings of about fourteen persons sitting at this table, eating duck and green peas and washing down the tasty food with glasses of cider, the glasses being replenished from two large jugs which stood in the middle of the table.

To the right of the hall was the sitting room, which was rarely used. Besides the couch, armchairs and usual furniture stood a glass case in which was mounted a stuffed badger which was one of my grandfather's trophies.

The stairs led from the hall to the first floor, on which there were five large bedrooms, and thence to a large garret which ran the whole length of the house. The garret was dark and gloomy and rather terrified me when I was a young child. It was used for storing apples and I rarely went there.

In the hall, opposite the front door, was a highly polished door with a gleaming brass handle and latch. This opened into a dark passage-way which led to the rear of the house and opened out into a kitchen-cum-living room of barn-like dimensions.

The usual enormous fireplace stood in the middle of one wall. On one side of it was a large copper or boiler and on the other side the door to the baking oven, which was bricklined, had a domed roof and was large enough for a person to squeeze into.

Racks holding sides of bacon were suspended from iron hooks fixed into the ceiling. A door led off from one side into the dairy where the cream was separated from the milk, the butter and cheese were made, and the more perishable foodstuffs were stored. Another door opened to the small paved yard, which in turn led into the cherry orchard. Above the living room and dairy was a large store-room.

On one side of the passage was the pantry, a room some eighteen feet by eight, and on the other side a door opened to the stone steps leading down to a damp, dark and clammy cellar which housed the hogsheads and casks of cider.

We entered the living room, where my aunt gave me an affectionate hug and then proceeded to pour out tea for us all. Soon there was the yapping of dogs and the sound of footsteps and the tap of a walking stick.

"That sounds like your grandpa coming," said my aunt. "Aren't you going to meet him?"

But I was already on my feet; I needed no second bidding. We were two of a kind, my grandfather and I, always ready for a joke or a bit of mischief. What one didn't think of, the other did — especially as I grew older.

"Hello, young man — you got here, then," he said to the little boy in his linen suit. He stooped down for me to kiss his leathery cheeks half covered with white-whiskered side burns.

"Hello, Grandpa," and I solemnly took his proffered hand to shake it.

"Not that one," he said, laughing. "Give me the other."

I was, and still am, left-handed in many things that I do and I invariably shook hands with my left one when I was small. Greetings over, he too came into the house for tea.

★ ★ ★

Quite a remarkable man was my grandfather. At the age of about sixty-five years, when most people were thinking of retiring, he had handed over his farm, with most of his stock and implements, to his son. He had then bought another farm — the one I was now visiting — and set about building up another thriving business.

As a boy he had had little or no schooling, for when he was supposed to be at school he usually played truant. Instead of attending the village school in Gloucestershire, where he was born, he used to "borrow" an old woman's donkey for the day. The outcome of his aversion to learning was that his knowledge of reading and writing was almost nil. Nonetheless, he was a very shrewd businessman.

At the age of fourteen he ran away from home and boarded a ship for Australia. Somehow or other he had managed to get himself a passage on a ship called the SS *London* and the promise of a job in the Australian outback. However, fate decreed that he was never to get there for, in the Bay of Biscay, a violent storm arose and the SS *London* was sent to her doom. The only survivors were grandpa and a few members of the crew who got themselves to safety on a raft.

He had led a very active life and had often been involved in some devilish prank or other, and had, on more than one occasion, proved his prowess in a bout of fisticuffs.

This art proved very valuable at one particular time.

He had a great friend who was a local magistrate. This administrator of the law had passed sentence on Harris, a well-known ruffian, for stealing and had sent him to prison for a spell. One market day, after his release from prison, Harris sought out the magistrate in the cattle market and, with much swearing and abuse, attacked him violently, swearing that he would kill him.

Grandpa rushed to his aid, the light of battle shining in his eyes, and with a couple of well-aimed blows floored the fellow and kept him subdued until the police took over. I recall the excitement with which my father related the episode to my mother when he returned from market on that particular day.

"Your dad made a name for himself today all right."

"Why, what happened?" asked my mother.

"You remember old Harris who was sent to clink by Idwal Jones, don't you?"

"Yes."

"Well, he came out a few days ago and today he came to the cattle market, found poor old Idwal and said he would finish him for good. I think he would have done it too if your dad hadn't been there. Idwal was in a mess, bleeding like a pig, and then up rushed your dad and really set about Harris."

"Go on!"

"He knocked him flat and kept him there until the police came and hauled him off to the station."

"Was Dad hurt at all?" asked my mother anxiously.

"Not a scratch on him, but I reckon if he hadn't been there, Harris would have ended up on the rope."

Not bad going, I thought, for a man in his seventies. Even in his eighties he was over six feet tall, broad and tough as nails. When he was about eighty-six and I was in my midteens, I used to spar with him but couldn't get within striking distance for fear of those granite-like fists.

Most school holidays I went to stay with my grandparents, who looked forward to my visit as much as I did.

Easter, Whitsun, summer and Christmas holidays brought different routines on the farm according to the season, but certain days of the week were set aside by the womenfolk for certain tasks. Thus Friday was churning day and Wednesday was baking day. Immediately after breakfast the fire was lit in the big baking oven. When the kindling wood was well ablaze, long logs of wood, the length of the oven, were thrown in and the fire was kept going until the brick lining glowed red-hot. Meanwhile the dough was being prepared and kneaded with the yeast and left to rise in front of the hot oven.

After lunch the oven was cleared of the wood ashes and wiped clean with a damp cloth. The dough was cut up into pieces to make twelve large loaves, with a special small loaf which was for me alone. There was also one for Hal if he was staying there at the same time. The glorious aroma of freshly baked home-made bread now began to fill the air. At last tea time arrived and there was my own loaf by my plate, still warm from the oven. The home-made butter, beautifully golden, just melted on the crusty bread and I almost gorged myself into a state of immobility.

★ ★ ★

I used to divide my time between my aunt, my grandmother and my grandfather. When I was with my grandfather we would either go fishing in the trout stream, do the rounds of the stock or spend time in his "study", as my grandmother called his retreat in the barn.

The barn was a very large T-shaped building. The top of the T was stacked to the rafters in the autumn with hay and straw. In the other part of the T was a particularly big oil engine which was used to provide power for driving the chaff-cutter and the mill for grinding the corn to make feeding stuffs for the animals. My grandfather had made a comfortable seat on the engine and here he used to sit and smoke a pipe of dark shag whilst I perched myself on a sack of oats and chatted away merrily. Also in this friendly community were three dogs and as many cats, all enjoying the social gathering in their various ways.

When I was about twelve years old one of my first acts on arriving at the farm was to make a pipe for myself. A piece of elderwood with the pith taken out provided the bowl, and a search amongst the hedgerows resulted in my finding a length of dead honeysuckle stem which was hollow. It was a simple matter, with the aid of grandpa, to make a small hole near the base of the elderwood so that the stem fitted snugly into place. The dried flowers of clover made my "tobacco" and this was sometimes supplemented by a pinch of shag from grandpa's pouch. We sat together in the "study", puffing contentedly and talking about nothing in particular.

"Don't you go near your gran when you go indoors," warned grandfather. "If she smells smoke on you she'll play old boots with me. So mind and keep your distance."

"Yes, of course I'll be careful," I promised, and took the advice so seriously that I was almost afraid to go near the house for hours afterwards. To make doubly sure, I would eat a piece of raw swede, thinking that this would clear my breath of the smell of smoking.

As we smoked and talked, the dogs, between spells of napping, jumped up to be fussed, whilst a tortoiseshell cat looked down on them from a privileged position on grandpa's shoulder. Background noises were provided by the rattle of the chain around the head of William the bull as he shook it in the cot next to the oil engine, the raucous cackle of the geese in the yard outside the barn door or the shrieking of a hen as she left the hay-loft where she had just laid an egg. Fainter sounds in the distance came from the cooing of the wild pigeons and the cawing of rooks from the tall trees which lined the brook at the bottom of the fields.

The farm was in an isolated spot. A few cottages and adjoining farms were the only other places of habitation, apart from the occasional tiny village and hamlet, for miles around. It was an event of some magnitude for a car to pass by, and when one did we dashed to the other end of the barn and peered through the cracks in the tall doors to see who it might be.

It was an exciting moment for me when the oil engine was started up for a session of corn-grinding and chaff-cutting. A few swings on the massive fly-wheel would get it going and it would phut-phut-phut-phut until the operation was completed. Then all was silent again. On one occasion nothing would induce it to start. My grandfather and the farmhand were baffled.

"It's no good, we must send for an engineer," said my grandfather. The farmhand got on his rickety old bicycle and set off down the road — I don't know where to — to send for an engineer.

A day or two later he turned up. It seemed that he only gave a glance at the machine. Then he pulled a hammer from his bag, gave it a sharp tap, and it started up without more ado.

"How much do I owe you?" asked grandpa.

"I reckon a couple of pounds will meet it," replied our expert visitor.

"A couple of pounds? But all you have done is just give it a tap," said grandpa.

"Aye, I know, but I'm not charging for the tap but for knowing where to tap," replied the engineer.

"I reckon that chap is a bit of a sharp 'un," said grandpa when he had gone on his way.

In those early days of the 1920s the toilet was situated at the end of the orchard, some fifty yards from the house. On winter nights when it was a sharp frost or it was wet and windy, the call of nature had to be strong indeed to induce one to brave the elements in order to make the pilgrimage to "Mrs Jones" or the "Houses of Parliament", as the privy was often called. To light the way and provide some cheerfulness during the visit, a hurricane lamp was taken along.

The privy was stone-built and was a family model since it was a three-seater — two for adults and one much lower for a child. There one could sit and meditate, tapping one's heels against the wooden box. A flowering cherry tree overhung the door, which had ventilation holes near the top. The seating was arranged over a trench and this led to a ditch running down the tall hedge which divided the orchard from the adjoining meadow.

On one occasion a piece of light-hearted drama was enacted in and around the privy. It seems that the maid had gone there one day. Suddenly the door burst open and, shrieking with terror, with skirts held high, she came running down the orchard to the house. On the other side of the tall hedge the farm labourer slunk off down the meadow with a sly grin on his face, leaving a long bean pole, with a bunch of nettles tied at one end, propped up against the hedge. What the maid thought and felt one can only guess!

In the early summer there were hundredweights of cherries to be gathered from the orchard. The birds appointed themselves as helpers on their own account and did considerable damage to the crop, from our point of view. Large birds, little birds, blackbirds, crows, magpies and jays infested the cherry orchard.

"Blast those birds," shouted Grandpa in exasperation, rushing out and letting fly with a double-barrelled twelve-bore in the direction where they were thickest.

A cloud of feathered miscreants arose from the trees, flapped off to the tall hedge of the orchard and perched there waiting . . . waiting . . . waiting. When all was quiet they came swooping back in twos and threes, sixes and dozens, until the trees were full of birds again and the crop of cherries diminished still further.

During cherry time my parents, brother and I, together with friends and their daughters from a neighbouring farm, went by horse and trap the three miles or so from my first home to gather cherries. On a bright Sunday morning we set off for the day and how memorable it was! At five years old I was madly in love with one of the daughters and I hadn't seen her since Friday when we walked home from my first seat of learning. When we arrived at my grandparents' home we were given the usual warm welcome and then everyone set about cherry-picking in earnest. A lot of cherries, pale yellow and blushing pink, were eaten at the same time, which left little room for the roast duck that my grandmother set before us when we were all seated at the long dining table. Nevertheless, justice was done to the fine spread and, after washing it down with glasses of cider, we were in no mood for further cherry-picking on a hot afternoon. The cherries were left to the birds.

One cherry time a rather amusing incident occurred. The wife of the neighbouring farmer came to pick some cherries. The family, maid and farmhand were sitting down to lunch in the back living room and from the table a view of part of the orchard was possible. Old John's wife was up a ladder propped against a tree in front of the window. The diners were watching her picking the fruit as they attended to the roast beef and vegetables. Suddenly it happened!

A rung in the ladder broke and old Polly slipped through the space between the rungs until she was suspended by her armpits. There she was dangling in mid-air, legs waving frantically backwards and forwards.

"Help me, help me!" she shrieked. "Help! I'm stuck."

Will, the labourer, rushed out to give assistance. But here was a fine problem! He couldn't get up the ladder to heave her up, and how could he get underneath to push her up without causing the lady acute embarrassment? Her long skirts were jammed up chest-high in the ladder rungs so that her only covering was a laced-up bodice, black stockings and knee-length open drawers. Will walked slowly around the scene of the mishap trying to decide how to find a way out of the predicament.

"Get me out, get me out," yelled Polly with more than a hint of panic in her voice.

"I dan know 'ow I be going to do it," replied Will, looking everywhere except at Polly.

"Get underneath and push my legs up," shouted old Polly, now throwing all caution to the winds and putting all sense of propriety to one side.

Bachelor Will gulped, took a deep breath and grasped Polly's legs firmly and heaved. Polly heaved as well and, with a concerted effort, she was finally free, down the ladder and skirts at ankle length again. She picked up her basket of cherries and, red-faced,

118

scuttled off home. Will stood for a few moments in a kind of trance, hypnotised by the sights he had seen, and then walked slowly back to the house to finish his interrupted lunch.

One Whitsun holiday during the early 1930s when I was staying with my grandparents, an event occurred in Monmouthshire which brought fear, tragedy and excitement and formed the main topic of conversation for several weeks afterwards amongst the local population. It also demonstrated the awesome force of nature when it is unleased in all its fury.

The day had dawned bright and sunny in late May and there was no indication of what lay before us. After tea one of the farmhands, a man of around forty, steady in his ways and with fixed intentions of what he wanted to do with his life, washed and changed into his best clothes to go and do a bit of courting. He lived in the farmhouse and earned the princely sum of eighteen shillings a week. He saved hard, for his ambition was to farm on his own account.

Dick pushed his bike out of the yard and set off to meet the woman who was to become his wife. As the evening wore on, the atmosphere became heavier and sultry and, as we made our rounds of the poultry houses to secure all doors against the attentions of nocturnal predators, ominous black clouds began to make their appearance on the horizon. After supper my grandparents and I went off to bed, leaving the door unbarred for Dick when he would return late at night.

There were rumblings of thunder as I dozed off to sleep. I couldn't have been asleep for long before I was suddenly brought to wakefulness by a terrific bang which seemed to shake the whole neighbourhood. The room was lit as if it was daytime and the yard could be seen quite clearly. Then the heavens seemed to open and the rain poured down in a ceaseless torrent.

"Is Dick back yet?" shouted my grandfather. "I'm worried about the foal."

One of the mares had given birth to a foal a few days earlier and this was no weather for it to be out so young. After what seemed an interminable time the sound of the yard gate being opened was heard between the successive claps of thunder. Grandpa was already at the window, calling to Dick.

"Dick, Dick, will you get the mare and foal in?"

"Yes, boss, I'm just going to do it."

Dick, already drenched to the skin after his long ride, went off down the road to the field. Soon the clip-clop of hooves was heard as mare and foal came to the stables, only too glad to be out of the deluge.

Despite the storm, I fell fast asleep and awoke next morning to find the sun shining again. Over breakfast the storm was the main topic of conversation.

"I'm thankful you got the foal in all right. Dick," said grandpa.

"Yes, so am I," added my grandmother. "But I was terrified with all that lightning."

"Aye 'twas bad. I admit I was mighty scared on the bike," said Dick. "I don't think I have ever known a storm like it."

Little did we know then what chaos it had created over the surrounding area. The first indication was given when we went down the fields to the brook. What was normally a small stream had become a raging torrent. It had uprooted quite large trees and swept everything before it. As these small tributaries joined larger streams to flow into the river Trothy, the flood had swelled to such an extent that bridges had either been swept away completely or were so badly damaged as to make them unsafe to use.

In Abergavenny streams and rivers had risen so rapidly that a great torrent swept through one of the streets, engulfing a row of houses, drowning several people and rendering many others homeless. A local state of emergency was set up to help those poor unfortunate people.

In this delightful countryside, life was very leisurely and there was "time to stand and stare", "time to stop at beauty's glance and watch her feet how they could dance". To my young mind the locals seemed ageless. Each year and each season of the year they appeared to be without change.

Amongst them were certain characters who stood out from the rest, and amongst these was Bill the postman. The point about Bill which fascinated me was his nose. I could hardly take my eyes off it when I was in his company. It was an extremely large, bulbous nose of a deep purple hue. Grandmother said it was due to the amount of drink which Bill consumed, for he was noted for his liking for alcohol in all its forms.

Bill's territory was far-reaching. His base post office was in Grosmont, some three miles away across the fields as the crow flies. How many miles Bill walked during the day delivering letters to the outlying farms and cottages I cannot say, but he arrived at my grandparents' farm at around eleven o'clock each morning.

He usually made a stop of about half an hour and came into the house to eat his mid-morning snack of bread and cheese. To refresh him even more, he always had a jug of cider to wash it down. Bill was a mine of information, and on his travels gossip stuck to him like flies to fly-paper.

"Good morning, postman," was how my grandmother greeted him as he appeared at the back door.

"Mornin', ma'am," replied Bill, taking off his peaked cap and seating himself in the high-backed wooden settle.

"You'll have a jug of cider with your bait?" asked grandmother, knowing full well what the answer would be.

"Yes, please, missus," said Bill, who would have been quite disappointed if he had gone without.

The routine preliminaries over, my grandmother pretended to be busy but was really waiting expectantly for the titbits of news which Bill had garnered on his way. He methodically unwrapped his bread and cheese, took a long draught of his cider and a bite of his bait.

Meanwhile Gran curbed her impatience and tried to look unconcerned, knowing that the news would begin to flow in Bill's good time.

"Very bad business," he muttered at length, almost to himself.

"What's bad business? asked Gran.

"'bout old Harris from Pant farm."

"Harris, postman? What about him?"

"Didn't you 'ear about 'im? Disappeared for two days. The police got up a search party but couldn't find any trace of 'im!"

"You don't say. I wonder where he's gone."

"Oh, they'm found 'im now. Young Jimmy Jones found 'im dead in the old dingle on the other side of the wood."

"No!" said Gran in a shocked voice.

"Aye, they reckoned 'e poisoned 'imself with strychinine!"

"Poor soul, whatever possessed him to do that?"

"Doan know, but they do tell me that the doctor did a post-mortem on 'im on the kitchen table and sent some of 'im away to be examined."

"But where did he get the poison?" asked my grandmother.

"I 'eard 'e 'ad it for killing moles."

"Well, I do declare! What a terrible thing to happen and how awful for his poor wife. Poor soul! Whatever will she do now? Have to sell the farm, I 'spose."

Silence reigned for a while, whilst Gran turned the tragedy over in her mind, and Bill munched his bread and cheese before launching the next bolt of hot news.

"Young Nancy Richards 'ave made a fine mess of things," said Bill in a matter-of-fact voice.

"Oh!" exclaimed Grandma, waiting for the fuller details.

"Aye, she's been running around with that young feller from Ty Hir and now I 'ear tell that she be got herself into trouble."

"Well, I can't say I'm surprised," replied my grandmother. "She was a proper young madam, flighty as an unbroke colt. I don't know what the world is coming to, I'm sure."

"And another thing," said Bill. "The bloke is taking her father to court because he 'aven't paid 'im 'is overtime. If the case goes 'is way, 'e'll 'ave quite a sum to come."

"I suppose with a baby on the way he's having to scratch together all the money he can get hold of to marry her," commented my grandmother.

Bill, who had by now finished the last crumbs and drained the jug dry, eased himself to his feet and picked up his cap.

"I wonder if you would post this letter for me?" asked Gran.

Bill took the letter, placed it in his bag, said his farewell and went on his way. Although this was his last delivery, he didn't usually go home but carried on down the road another half a mile to the public house, the one referred to by my grandmother as a "den of sin".

Sometimes he passed by on his homeward journey during late afternoon or late evening. Sometimes he returned when we were all abed. Then his presence on the return journey was heralded by the barking of the dogs in the barn. In the stillness of the night the barking, punctuated by the hooting of an owl, echoed round the old grey buildings.

When I was in my middle teens, Hal went to live with my grandparents to help run the farm and, under the direction of my grandfather, who was now over eighty years of age, was rapidly becoming efficient in farm management.

One morning, after breakfast, Hal was walking down the road by the farm to check on the stock in the lower fields when he met old John, who lived at the next farm down the road. The old chap, now in his late seventies, had rarely moved from the neighbourhood except to go to the local cattle market and he had been to the seaside only once in his life. About the only evidence of modern technology in his possession was a radio and he had not had that very long.

"Mornin', and 'ow be you this mornin'?" he asked my brother.

"Not too bad, thanks," replied my brother. "It's a nice morning and it looks as if we will have a nice day."

But old John couldn't agree with this opinion.

"No, no, 'e said on the wireless that we be goin' t'ave some rain," said John.

"Well, on the eight o'clock news the forecast was fine and dry," replied my brother.

"No, 'e said it was going to rain," said John, quite determined to have his way.

"Well, I didn't hear that anyways," contradicted Hal.

"Ah!" exclaimed old John, his eyes lighting up with inspiration. "But you be got a different wireless to what we be got."

At this, Hal went on his way, wondering if his ears had deceived him.

Grandpa was very fond of a game of cards. He taught Hal and me to play a number of games, including some typical gambling ones. On these occasions we never allowed to play for money as my grandmother rather frowned on the whole business and thought cards were an evil. To put some element of excitement into the game, we played for dried beans as stakes.

During the dark evenings of the winter holidays, as soon as the tea table was cleared, grandpa, the farmhand, Hal and I would settle down for an evening of nine card don. We cut for partners and the game was on. During the playing of some hands, the tension could be cut with a knife. Gran sat by the fire reading the *Hereford Times* and, no doubt, thinking what a lot of childish males she had around her.

During this period I was at my fourth seat of learning and had begun to acquire some knowledge of chemistry, particularly the parts of interest to schoolboys, such as how to make stink-bombs. On one visit I took with me some pieces of iron sulphide and some dilute hydrochloric acid and I thought that it would be fun to try it out one evening. My brother had been informed of the devilish plot and was looking forward to the prank.

126

Between a hand of cards, when they were being dealt, I excused myself, went behind the high-backed settle and tipped the acid into a small bottle containing some iron sulphide. I then put the bottle in a dark corner and went back to the game.

As we played, the smell of rotten eggs began to pervade the atmosphere. Grandpa wrinkled up his nose and looked sideways at Will the farmhand. He said nothing. He looked at my brother and then at me but still said nothing. Will tried to appear unconcerned, whilst grandmother glanced furtively at the players from behind her newspaper.

Not only was the air full of hydrogen sulphide but it was also full of suspicion. Meanwhile, the smell increased and feet began to shuffle in embarrassment. It was as much as Hal and I could do to keep a straight face. Grandpa's looks became fiercer and more direct. Who was the guilty person? At last he could stand it no longer and decided that the direct approach was the only one.

"Have you done anything, Will?" he almost shouted. Will looked most upset.

"No, I haven't," he retorted indignantly.

"Where's that damned cat?" roared grandpa. "Turn the dirty varmint out."

Up jumped everyone to look for the cat, which was sleeping peacefully on the sofa. It was rudely awakened and hurled out through the back door, which was left open to clear the offensive smell. During the confusion I took the opportunity to throw the bottle and its contents into the orchard as I felt things were getting a little out of hand.

Although she couldn't understand what had really happened, I rather fancy that my grandmother thought that I had something to do with it and that too much learning wasn't a good thing.

"I feel quite sick," she said huffily. "I'm going to bed and you can all get your own suppers."

We sat there sheepishly for a while and then decided to call it a day.

During the Christmas holidays it was customary to take a day off from work on the farm to have some shooting. One bright frosty day, after the essential jobs had been done, the ferret was taken out of his cage, popped into a little sack, and with pockets full of cartridges we were off for a day's sport.

On the last Christmas holidays of my school days it was arranged that we would have a shoot. But circumstances decreed that the usual party was not to be. We were almost ready to go, when a timber buyer appeared at the farm gate. Grandpa had decided to sell some timber standing on the farm and, today of all days, the valuer had come to sort out and mark the suitable trees.

My brother and the farmhand went off with the valuer, leaving grandpa and me together. Although he was now eighty-six years of age he was determined not to be done out of his sport.

"Come on," he said. "Get the gun and ferret and let's be off."

With the double-barrelled twelve-bore under my arm and the ferret wriggling in her bag, we were on our way, two of the dogs dancing around our legs excitedly.

"Let's go down to the ox-pasture. There's a good warren there and I noticed a lot of trade around the holes."

By "trade" he meant fresh earth and marks on the ground where many rabbits had recently been. He plodded along beside me, his long walking stick prodding the ground as he went. Eventually we reached the warren, which was a mound of ground bounded by a stream on one side and densely covered by bushes.

The ferret was released from the bag near one of the holes. She arched her back, sniffed the air and, with the characteristic undulating motion of the stoat family, disappeared into the ground.

We stood back, tense with expectation, watching a number of entrances to the warren all at the same time. There was a thumping of the ground and rabbits seemed to pop up from all directions.

"Watch out, there he goes," shouted Grandfather, dancing about in his excitement and waving his stick in the direction of the rabbits. The gun was hardly to my shoulder when I squeezed the trigger.

Bang! Bang! and two rabbits bit the dust.

"There's another! There's another!" yelled Grandpa before I had time to reload.

"Hi-yi-yi! After him, Rover," shouted Grandpa as one dived into a bush.

The dogs needed no second bidding. One was into the bush, whilst the other rushed around to the other

129

side, waiting for the unfortunate creature to emerge. These dogs were old hands at this game and worked as a team.

Rabbits were still rushing out and cartridges were being expended as quickly as I could reload. Some got away. Good luck to them!

Then all was quiet. After a while the ferret appeared at the mouth of the burrow and just stood there sniffing the air. I took one of the dead rabbits and dangled it just in front of her to entice her into the open. It was then an easy matter to grab her by the neck and pop her back into her little sack.

As it looked as though a heavy storm would soon be upon us, we gathered up our spoils, called the dogs and set off for home. We were well satisfied with our couple of hours of excitement.

Grandpa and I were always the best of pals — he used to call me his buddy — and we were always full of fun and mischief.

He retained this sense of humour until he died aged ninety-three, despite suffering a stroke in his late eighties — much to his annoyance.

CHAPTER ELEVEN

Cheese and Cider

Much of today's food is sadly lacking in flavour. This has been an insidious and creeping effect as more processed vegetables and meat made their appearance. No doubt this is a necessary evil since a growing world population has to be fed. But what a joy it would be to get the tastebuds in contact with the home-grown, home-made foods which I enjoyed, but did not fully appreciate, as a child.

It was customary for my grandfather, before World War I, to kill a beast each year and salt the meat in barrels to provide a ready source for boiled beef and carrots dishes. These were so popular then that lyrics have been written about them. We did not kill a beast at my home but only a pig each year.

One day of the week, usually Friday, was set aside for butter-making. Twice each day, morning and evening, the cows were milked and the cream separated from the milk. During the week several large panfuls of thick cream accumulated, and this was placed in the churn, which had been thoroughly washed and scalded with boiling water.

The older churns consisted of a barrel which was rotated on its horizontal axis. These were later replaced with more efficient churns which were rotated end over end, and had paddles inside to agitate the cream and a small glass window to observe how the conversion from cream to butter was proceeding. As I recall, the process was rather a temperamental one and depended very much on the state of the weather. Sometimes butter would form in half an hour or less, but in very hot weather it might take up to an hour or longer. It was quite hard work rotating the churn, with something like a quarter of a hundredweight of cream inside it, for such a time.

On occasions the cream would attach itself to the sides of the churn and centrifugal force would tend to keep it there. It then became necessary to rotate the churn backwards and forwards in jerky movements to dislodge it. In the early stages the cream made a gentle swishing sound as the churn was rotated but, as the conversion got under way, the sound gradually diminished and it became easier to rotate the churn. Then, quite suddenly, as the butter began to form, the plop of butter in buttermilk could be distinctly heard and the churn became heavier to turn, since the twenty pounds or so of butter fell to the bottom of the barrel. The glass window, which had previously been covered with cream, was now clear and spattered with small pieces of golden yellow butter.

The next stage in the process was to drain off the buttermilk, which was used to make the most delightful cream cheeses imaginable. Cold water was then added to the churn and the butter washed several times. This was most important in hot weather to harden it, otherwise the subsequent operations became almost impossible to carry out.

The implement used to process the butter was called a "butter-worker" and consisted of a shallow wooden trough about six feet by two feet on a stand, capable of holding water, and a wooden roller with deep serrated ridges which could be moved along the trough with a handle. This rolled out the butter and ridged it so that salt could be added. The butter was rolled in alternate directions until the salt had been intermixed and all surplus water had been removed.

It was then weighed into pound and half-pound lots on a pair of scales and made into blocks with a pair of butter pats. These were carved with ornamental facings so that the finished pats of butter finished up with elaborate patterns of ferns, cows or whatever design the maker was wont to use. The finished product was then stacked on slabs of slate to keep it cool until it was taken to market.

The whole operation was carried out under scrupulously clean conditions and the scales were checked at regular intervals by the Inspectorate of Weights and Measures.

During the summer months my mother, like most other farmers' wives in the district, made a sufficient quantity of cheeses to last the whole year through. The milk, which was placed in a large, glazed earthenware pan, was curdled by adding rennet. After a time the semi-solid mass of soft white curds was cut into chunks and put into a sort of large colander for the whey to drain off. The curds were crumbled and placed in a vat which had been lined with a cheese cloth. The cloth was folded over the cheese and the top put on the vat. Two or three vats were put in the cheese-press under pressure to squeeze out as much of the whey as possible. This gave a cheese which had good keeping qualities and a flavour which improved with age. After some days the cheese would be finally turned out of its vat and left to mature on the dairy shelves.

Every day the cheeses were taken out of the vats and clean cloths substituted for the used ones; this was to prevent souring. This part of the cheese-making was always of interest to Hal and me. As the vat lid was pressed down into the vat, a rim of cheese formed around the top of the main bulk, and before the clean cloth was put on it this surplus rim was trimmed off. The trimmings were delicious. Hal and I stood by my mother like young fledglings, mouths open to receive the tasty morsels. We swallowed the long trimmings as the fledglings would worms.

These cheeses varied in texture and flavour according to the state of their maturity. When comparatively fresh they tasted like a Caerphilly cheese, and as they matured they became firmer and sometimes crumbly; yet others developed blue veins through them.

During the winter months they were eaten with great enjoyment with celery or pickled onions for supper by a blazing log fire in the soft glow of the lamplight. By late spring they had become so rich that they almost walked off the table.

On the farm a couple of orchards were stocked entirely with trees which bore cider apples and cider pears. The autumnal gales brought the fruit crashing to the ground and what was left on the trees was finally shaken off the branches.

On Saturdays Hal and I were set to work to pick up the fruit and place it in heaps ready for collection by cart. This was a most tedious and uninteresting job and we did our best to get out of it.

"Why do we have to pick up the rotten old apples?"

"It's a job you can very well do," said my father. "So get on with it. You like cider, don't you?"

True, we liked a tot of cider, but whether we did or not, this was our command and we had no choice in the matter. The dreary task was finally finished and the day for cidermaking was at last upon us.

The cider mill was in a shed of its own and consisted of a large circular stone trough around which the huge millstone was rotated by a horse harnessed to a wooden beam which passed through the centre of the stone. The poor old horse trudged patiently around and around all day long whilst buckets and buckets of apples were thrown into the trough.

When a quantity had been mashed, the pulp was placed on to a type of coconut matting called "hairs", the edges of the matting wrapped around the pulp and the process repeated until a number of "hairs" had been built up one upon the other. These were assembled in a press and when pressure was applied the clear juice flowed into a container which was emptied into casks of one hundred and twenty gallons capacity. Water was added so that the final product would not be too potent after fermentation.

"I do hope they are putting in enough water," said my mother with a worried look on her face. "They didn't put enough in last year, it was far too strong."

Sound apples, rotten apples, half rotten apples — all went into the brew. On some farms the water came from the pond in the farmyard where the ducks and geese swam and was almost the colour of chocolate from the mud stirred up from the bottom. I have also heard tell of the odd rat that fell into the must and was consumed during fermentation. Some farmers added a few pounds of raw beef to the fermenting must, saying that it gave body to the drink.

The pithy residue left after the juice had been squeezed out of the pulp was stacked to dry out and used as fuel for the fire in much the same way as peat is burnt.

The must was left for some six weeks to ferment and then the casks were securely bunged to exclude all air.

The cider, like the cheese, changed with age. When fresh it was a deliciously sweet drink but became much drier with keeping until, after a year, it was almost vinegar. However, many wonderful health-giving properties have been attributed to cider vinegar so perhaps this is the reason that farmers and their workers had such ruddy complexions.

"I think I'll tap the cider," said my father one morning with an air of excitement and expectancy in his voice. This was the moment of truth. How had the brew turned out? I can remember toddling off to the cider house, holding his hand with one hand and a cup in the other to take part in the tasting ceremony.

With one sharp blow of the hammer, the tap was in the barrel and the nectar began to flow. Half a cup was my ration — this being considered enough for a four-year-old. I must confess that I took more kindly to cider than to milk. This was man's stuff!

The cider house was quite a social centre as neighbours and passers-by often dropped in for a chat over a glass or two or more.

When fermentation was over we usually bottled a quantity. The corks were wired in the bottle as the liquid had a rather restless nature and required careful containment.

Fresh cider was a very effective aperient and, quite apart from its intoxicating effect, needed to be drunk with care to prevent embarrassing situations arising. Cider which had been bottled in late autumn made a very pleasant drink if left until the following spring or summer and shared champagne's bubbly nature.

Perry, treated in the same way, also made a very pleasant drink. One had to take considerable care in opening the bottle since it was so eager to be released from its glass prison that it often ended up on the ceiling.

At the local flower and agricultural shows bottled cider was one of the regular exhibits and my uncle invariably carried off first prize. After the judging had taken place and the exhibition tents had been thrown open to the public, much hilarity could be heard in the corner of the tent where the cider exhibits were.

The local yokels made a point of converging in this direction to judge the quality of the prize-winning beverage for themselves.

"There's no doubt about it, 'Ole 'Arry be got some good cider this year. 'ave some more, William," said old Farmer Bailly, his red beard glistening with spilt cider.

The more respectable farmers' wives, who were examining the butter, cheese and poultry exhibits, shot deprecating glances in the direction of the revellers.

"Disgusting lot," remarked Mrs Evans.

"Trust old Bailly to make a pig of himself," added Miss Pritchard, nicking a piece of butter on her thumb nail and stroking it with her tongue. "A bit too much salt in this I would say, but then Mrs Williams always did overdo the salt. Don't like salty butter."

But the cider connoisseurs weren't interested in butter. The party was getting rowdier and would continue to do so until only empty bottles remained.

Rough cider was one of the main drinks on the farms in Monmouthshire when I was young. It was drunk during the morning, for mid-day lunch, during the afternoon and often at night. The farm labourers always took a bottle with them when they went to work in the fields, and two quart jugs were always on the table for lunch. On winter evenings at supper time it was a custom to put a poker into the fire until it became red-hot and then to plunge it into a jug of cider, which was then drunk as a nightcap. This was said to be a cure for colds. On reflection I think it was just another excuse to drink cider!

Large quantities were consumed during the hay-making season. This was hot work and the dryish quality made an excellent thirst-quencher. When one was working hard in the hot days of summer the intoxicating effect was somewhat nullified by sweating profusely, but with lack of exercise it had a decided soporific effect and this almost had dire consequences for me on one occasion when I was staying with my grandparents during a summer holiday.

I had had two or three glasses of a rather potent brew with my lunch and had then taken one of the horses and a mechanical rake to gather up the hay. The rake had a seat on it and the horse was driven with reins, rather as a horse and trap was driven.

The day was hot and my stomach was full after a good farmhouse lunch. The monotonous rattle of the rake and its swaying to and fro, combined with the effect of the cider, lulled me into a state of somnolence. My head began to nod whilst the horse plodded remorselessly on. Suddenly I awoke with a bang, having hit the ground behind the horse's hooves and in front of the spikes of the rake. Fortunately for me, the horse stopped short and I was able to scramble out of harm's way. For a while after that I was on the verge of signing the pledge.

I fancy that Grandpa's cider was more potent than that which we made at my own home.

The local brewer was a friend and Grandpa used to obtain rum casks from his brewery. His cider went into these casks and I can only suppose that a drop of rum was left in the cask and also soaked into the wood when it left the brewery for the farm. Anyway, it was most noticeable that those who drank Grandpa's cider soon acquired the complexions of turkey-cocks.

CHAPTER TWELVE

The Fat Pig

An annual event on most farms and in many cottages which had a paddock was the killing of a fat pig for bacon.

For some weeks the pig was fattened on a diet of barley meal or flaked maize with gallons of swill. The thick stodgy mixture was greedily swallowed by the pig, which grew fatter and fatter with each succeeding day. This was the only time I saw a pig with a double chin!

The weight of a pig was reckoned in so many "score", a score being twenty pounds. Whenever neighbours called on one another, the visitor was taken to see the fat pig and asked to judge its weight.

"When are you killing the pig?"

"Next week, I think he'll be ready by then. Come and have a look and tell me how much he weighs."

A shrewd eye sizes him up.

"I reckon he'll go about eighteen score," says one.

"Nearer twenty, I'd say," says another.

"Davy Lloyd reckons the fat pig will turn twenty score," said my father one evening.

"I hope he's not too fat," replied my mother. "You know we can't eat a lot of fat bacon."

"I'll write to Ted Owen tonight and see if he can come next week," announced my father.

Ted Owen was the itinerant butcher who travelled the neighbourhood butchering pigs for a fee of a few shillings. The following week Ted appeared on his bicycle at the farm gate, his implements of slaughter in a canvas bag slung from the crossbar.

A wooden bench was brought into the yard and all was made ready for the dastardly deed to be done. I stayed in the house whilst this was going on. I wasn't averse to taking part in a day's shooting but this was too cold-blooded, too deliberate and unsporting for my temperament. The poor victim didn't stand a chance.

It was dragged from its sty squealing with terror or protest, I knew not which, but squealed loudly it did. Three strong men heaved it on to the bench and held it whilst the cold-hearted butcher cut its throat. The squealing grew fainter and fainter as the poor creature's life ebbed away until all was quiet. Then, and only then, did I venture into the yard to watch the rest of the proceedings.

Nowadays it is illegal to slaughter animals in this way, and not before time either. They are now slaughtered under properly supervised and humane conditions.

The next stage was to get rid of the bristles. A layer of straw was placed on the ground and the pig put on top of it. The animal was then covered with more straw, which was then fired. It was then turned over on to its other side, which was burned likewise.

It was now necessary to scrub off the burnt bristles since the white skin was blackened by the singeing. The butcher had home-made gadgets for this purpose. They consisted of rectangular tins which had holes punched in them from the inside, thus making the outer surface of the metal rough and serrated. Straps to slip over the back of the hand completed the rough tools. Then with buckets of water the butcher set to work to scrub the skin clean. When this was completed he cut off the end of the pig's tail and threw it some distance away.

Turning to me he said, "Now then, young fella, what do you say the distance is from the pig's snout to the end of his tail?"

I studied the pig for a moment and replied, "I should think it's about six feet."

This reply sent the butcher into fits of raucous laughter.

"You 'aven't got much idea of measurement, 'ave you?" he said. "I would say it's all of fifteen feet."

I looked at him in bewilderment, thinking that I wasn't all that stupid.

"There's the end of his tail over there," he said, pointing to the spot where he had thrown the tip.

"Ah yes, very funny," I said, trying not to show my annoyance at being caught.

Clever fellow that!

I think that he must have tried that one on at every farm he went to as a regular routine. He tried it with me again the following year but I was ready for him the next time.

The scrubbing completed, the pig was put on a ladder and secured by its hind quarters to one end. The ladder was propped against a wall so that the head hung downwards. The intestines, heart, lungs and liver, together with the other offal, was removed and placed in enamel pans. Often one or more of the neighbours came to collect the intestines and take them to the nearby brook for a preliminary cleaning, then to their cottages for a final preparation before cooking. Some people are very partial to chitterlings.

Then with much heaving, the ladder and pig were dragged into the dairy and the pig suspended, head downwards, from the ceiling. There it was left for three days for the carcase to cool before it was cut up into its various parts.

When Ted Owen had washed and gulped down a couple of glasses of cider, he gathered up his tools and went on his way to his next pig-sticking appointment.

"Well, so long now, see you on Friday evening," he shouted as he wheeled his bicycle through the farm gate.

We got tea over quickly on Friday evening and sat waiting for Ted to put in his appearance. The barking of the dogs and the clump of hob-nailed boots in the yard heralded his approach. Soon, with his flannel shirt sleeves rolled up above his elbows, he was setting about his task.

The bench was brought in and the carcase laid upon it. The dismembering was carried out methodically. First the head was cut off, then the trotters, then the chine was removed to give the two sides, which were

144

each treated in turn. The layers of fat were taken out and put on one side to melt down to make lard. The ribs and meaty portions were deftly cut out to provide fresh pig-meat. This meat, when roasted, had a delicious flavour and was much tastier than the pork derived from a younger pig.

The remaining sides, with the hams and shoulders, were then ready for salting to make bacon. During the preceding days my mother had powdered down large blocks of salt in readiness. A layer of salt was placed on the thick slate slabs in the dairy and on to this was laid one of the sides. Saltpetre and pepper were rubbed well into the parts around the ham and shoulder bones, in addition to the salt, to prevent invasion by the bacon weevil. The side was covered with a further layer of salt and then the second side placed on top of that. The process was repeated with salt, pepper and saltpetre. After a fortnight the sides were reversed, fresh salt added where necessary, and left another fortnight.

The salt was then wiped off and the sides suspended on a bacon rack from the ceiling for them to dry. When dry, they were cut to provide two hams, two shoulders and the middle cuts of bacon, which were stored in large wooden boxes. This provided us with delicious food throughout the year, boiled, fried or grilled, hot with parsley sauce and boiled parsnips or cold with salads in the summer.

Having disposed of the sides, the butcher next turned his attention to dissecting the head. First he cut off the ears. Then he gouged out the eyes. Handing one of them to me he said. "Here you are, young 'un. Put that on a piece of newspaper and tell me what you can see."

I did as he asked and I was astonished with what I saw.

"Gosh!" I said in amazement. "It's like a magnifying glass." The small letters of print were magnified several times.

"There now, what do you think of that?" asked Ted Owen, and went on to say, "Do you know why pigs are afraid of people and why they don't attack them?"

"No," I said, looking at him for a further explanation.

"Think, boy, think."

"I don't know."

"Well, you've seen how that eye magnifies."

"Yes."

"Well, a pig's eye magnifies us and we look much bigger to a pig than we really are."

"Is that so?" I asked, thinking that Ted Owen was no mug after all.

I can't recall for how long I believed this but I know that for some time I was a Goliath to pigs and that this superior knowledge gave me plenty of Dutch courage.

When the ears and eyes had been removed, the head was split in half with the aid of saw and chopper. This operation revealed the brains. These were scooped out into a basin and when fried made a very tasty dish, as did the tongue after boiling. The two cheeks were salted down for future use. These were stuffed with seasoning and roasted. In fact there was little waste as all the bits and pieces, properly cooked, made tasty dishes; and

146

these were not a once-a-year treat either. There was more than one family could eat, and so the annual pig-killings amongst my relations was spread out between January and March and there was an exchange of meat and offal between the families. In this way there was no waste and a fairly regular supply during this period.

The late winter was chosen, for the weather was colder and there was less risk of the meat going to waste as there was no refrigeration available in the country areas, there being no electricity in those parts.

When the butcher had been paid his five shillings fee and had departed, there was still much to be done. The hard fat which the pig had stored up had to be melted down to make the lard, which was used during the coming year for making cakes and pastries. The fat was cut up into lumps about an inch square and a quantity put into a large iron pot. This was heated on a stove until it began to boil.

"Just you keep away from the stove. If that boiling fat upsets over you it will scald you to death," warned my mother.

I kept my distance and watched the goings-on out of harm's way. The bubbling, boiling contents of the pan were stirred with a wooden spoon and the heating continued until each lump had truly melted. It was finally strained through a muslin cloth. To squeeze out as much of the lard as possible, the ends of the muslin cloth were gathered together and each end twisted in opposite directions, rather like wringing out a sheet on washing day.

A mass of protein material remained in the cloth. When this cooled it became crisp and could be disintegrated into small pieces. These were called "scrutchings" and had a delightful flavour all of their own. It makes my mouth water just thinking of them.

Two other products of the pig were brawn and faggots. Bony parts of the head were boiled until the meat fell off them and then the meat, which contained gelatinous material, was compressed. Brawn eaten cold with pickles was delicious.

I often played a part in making the faggots. The pig's liver was firstly boiled and then minced. This was mixed with a quantity of breadcrumbs and minced onions. The mixture was then made up into balls, which were wrapped in pieces of the "apron", the thin membrane which covered the pig's belly. These were placed in roasting pans for cooking. The appetising smell of faggots filled the air and set all our mouths watering. What a time this was for eating!

Although I didn't realise it at the time, the killing of the pig was part of my education, for I learnt at first hand quite a lot about animal physiology.

CHAPTER
THIRTEEN

Seats of Learning — Two

In September 1926 we moved to another farm about five miles from Pontypool. While the move was being effected I went to stay with relations in Bridgend. I always enjoyed going to stay with my aunt and uncle and came to regard their house as almost a second home.

Meanwhile my brother had written me to say that he had already made new friends. We later found that they were not so friendly and that they came from a rather peculiar family. The father went under the name of "the Major" and they lived in a small house which had a very large board in the front which had painted on it "H. WILLS, BUILDER AND CONTRACTOR". No one could ever remember "Major" Wills doing any building or contracting, or, in fact, any work at all.

Once, when we were on our way home from school, we were approached by a man enquiring if we knew where Major Wills lived. One of our companions had an immediate and perfect answer to the question.

"Go down this road, mister, until you come to a big board, and behind the board is a little house and that is where Major Wills lives."

He kept goats in the back garden, which was overgrown with weeds. Now it is often said that dog owners grow to look like their dogs or dogs grow to look like their owners. Thus a dowager lady with her Pekinese, an elegant miss with her pampered poodle and a solid tweed-clad gentleman with his bull terrier fit together respectively.

Mrs Wills looked just like one of her nanny goats, even to the detail of having a few hairs on the end of her chin. The effect was so pronounced that I fully expected her to bleat instead of talk.

Just after we moved into our new farm my father had a hair-raising experience. He had taken the big wagon to collect a few remaining pieces of equipment from our previous home and had set out in the late afternoon on the eighteen-mile return journey.

It had been raining hard for a few days and the river Usk was in full flood. It was almost dark when he reached the bridge over the river, which had risen during the day, and the swirling brown waters were now rushing over the road. There was no other way across the river for miles either way and he urged the chestnut mare into the flood, thinking that it was only a foot or so deep. Bright gallantly plunged forward, eager to be home, and was soon floundering up to her belly in the angry torrent.

She began to falter, the wagon began to sway, and for a few dreadful moments it seemed that horse, wagon and driver would be swept away. Both realised the imminent danger and man and beast, who had worked so closely over the years, made the supreme effort. With muscles stretched to the limit and lungs almost at bursting point, the gallant chestnut struggled on. Gradually the level of the waters began to drop and, at last, dry land was reached. A pause for the horse to recover her breath and for my father to recover his composure; then they were off on the last leg of their journey home.

My mother was getting worried by the lateness of the hour but was unaware of the danger which he had encountered and was indeed thankful to see him safely home.

During September I was taken to our new home. It had previously belonged to a retired army officer who was known locally as a gentleman farmer. He had had a bailiff who had run the farm for him in rather an haphazard manner. The bailiff lived in a bungalow on the farm. The farmhouse itself had twelve rooms, excluding the large cool dairy and — what luxury! — a bathroom with a flush lavatory upstairs. There was so much to explore, so many nooks and crannies, and yet it was all so strange, an alien place indeed. Not home yet, no roots firmly in the ground, and more unknowns to come with the new school awaiting us in the morning.

When my father took us to introduce us to the headmaster, it was with surprise that we found that they were friends of years ago. The school was much bigger than the previous one and was situated in the village. In fact this part of Monmouthshire was much more densely populated. We were no longer in isolation, for the lines of communication were much better developed, the regular hourly bus service between Abergavenny and Pontypool and the main railway line from Birmingham to South Wales providing alternative means of transport.

There was a general stores and a sweet shop with such a variety of goodies as to make one's mouth water. It was a rare treat to be able to have twopence, to push open the door with its loud bell and dawdle over the momentous decision of what to buy. Would it be gob-stoppers or nougat or a bottle of pop? Pop came in glass bottles which were sealed, not by corks, but by a glass marble, and it was a work of art to push the marble into the bottle without losing too much of the precious fizzy drink. Sometimes Hal and I pooled our resources and had a half a bottle of pop each and twopenny-worth of sweets between us.

There was a builder's yard and carpenter's shop, where the local undertaker carried out his profession. Adjacent to this was the smithy. We used to stand and watch him at his craft either on our way home or during the lunch hour. The clang of hammer on anvil and hot iron echoed around the village and the pungent smell of burning hooves made us wrinkle our noses. No village is complete without its pub and this was situated near the bus stop on the main road. The drinking members of the neighbourhood found this a convenient shelter when waiting for a bus. It also had a back door for Sunday use, since all public houses were officially closed then. As the nearest police station was some three miles away, it did a fair unofficial trade on a Sunday.

The headmaster had three children, a daughter and two sons. The latter became good friends of my brother and myself and, I must confess, I went a bit gooey-eyed at the daughter, who was much older than me. The standard of teaching was high at this time but, unfortunately, this did not last long. Our headmaster was to take over a much bigger school in Pontypool.

Teachers and pupils were sad to see them go, and for a period we had a Mr Stark as our acting head. He, too, was a good master and a kindly man and very deceptive as regards his physical strength. There was an unpleasant boy who went under the name of Blubber. How he got this name no-one seemed to know, but I can only suppose it was because he was fat and awkward. He was also idle and shirked his work whenever he could.

One day Mr Stark had been keeping an eye on him.

"Boy, what are you eating?" he asked Blubber.

"Nuffin', sir."

"Don't lie to me. Open your mouth."

Blubber's mouth was full of toffee.

"You'll stay in during the break and do some arithmetic."

"But, but, sir."

"Silence, boy. Next time it will be the cane."

We all went out to play and were noisily minding our own business when there was a great commotion outside the school porch. Out rushed Blubber with Mr Stark after him.

"Come back at once!"

"I won't, I won't, you're an old —"

By now Mr Stark was within arm's length of Blubber, who suddenly whipped round and hacked Mr Stark on the shin.

All the other activity in the playground stopped to make way for this interesting digression. Mr Stark's arm shot out, and Blubber was grabbed by the scruff of his neck, lifted bodily from the ground and hauled off into the classroom.

"You little devil, I'll teach you not to kick people."

Roars of anguish emerged, and when we returned to our desks Blubber was still blubbering. We looked at Mr Stark with new eyes after this.

Our next permanent head was a Mr Sober, but his name was the complete opposite of his behaviour. He was a chronic alcoholic and was seldom sober in fact. As soon as opening time had come, the class was set some work to do.

"I have to go out for a while, so I want you to do some composition by the time I get back," was a usual remark as he hurried out of the classroom.

After a few weeks his class became accustomed to this instruction and also realised that when he did return he would have no interest in them or anything else.

There was a garden attached to the school house, and also one which was used to teach boys some rudiments of horticulture. When Mr Sober returned for the afternoon session, the boys of his class, providing the weather was suitable, were sent to work in one of the gardens and the girls were requested to do needlework. If the weather was unsuitable, he would sit behind his desk, face flushed, eyes glazed, and speak to the class with a slurring tongue. One could barely understand what he was saying and not many cared.

Most of the children regarded school as a dreadful chore and were only too eager to while away the time until they could leave and take a job. The standard of teaching from a drunken master and unqualified women teachers was so poor that few minds were stimulated enough to want to ask the question "Why?" Fortunately, my parents did something about this situation before I developed into a complete moron.

Not far from the school ran the Newport-Brecon canal, known locally as "The Cut". It was a delightful place in summer, with trees overhanging the side opposite the towpath. Water lilies blossomed on the placid waters and dragon flies flitted their colourful way across the water, darting hither and thither. Shoals of roach drifted lazily through the sunlit waters, disappearing from view as they swam into shadows cast by the overhanging trees. On fine days we used to go to the canal during the lunch break and eat our sandwiches.

155

Some of the older boys stripped off their clothes and swam in the canal and, to dry themselves, ran up and down the bank in the hot sun. The girls who were present thought this great fun and blatantly studied the physical differences between the sexes, giggling dirtily.

The canal bridges were narrow and humpbacked, the towpath running under the curve of the arch. One day a barge approached, drawn by a huge horse which must have stood about twenty-five hands. When the horse came to the bridge he stopped in his tracks.

"Gid-up, blast you," roared the bargee.

But no amount of shouting would make the horse move.

"Well, dang me, he be too big to get under. 'is 'ead is too 'igh," said the bargee.

We had been watching closely and one bright lad came up with a solution to the problem.

"Hey mister, why don't you get a spade and dig a bit out of the towpath? The horse could get under then."

"Don't be a young fool," replied the bargee. "It's 'is 'ead that won't go under, not 'is feet."

In the same way as there are seasons for cricket, tennis, football and hockey, so there were seasons for the games which we children used to play. For a certain period whip and top would be the rage and then this would be followed by hoops and then marbles and, in the autumn, by conkers.

A hoop was a circle of wrought iron, varying in diameter from two feet to perhaps three feet. It was propelled by smacking it, when rolling, with a stick or pushing it with a piece of iron rod which had a hook at one end. Boys who couldn't persuade the local blacksmith to make one for them through lack of copper coinage would scrounge an old bicycle wheel, which was then pushed along with a piece of stick.

This was good healthy exercise, for in the hoop season we ran miles in a day. It seems that the space age has ousted hoops for good!

We had to make our own amusements, particularly in the country, where visits to the moving pictures in the town were few and far between. Yet we were never bored, there being so much to do and so many things to interest us.

My brother and I collected birds' eggs and over a few years we had obtained about seventy species. We took one egg only from each nest and did not, as some boys did, rob the nests. The egg was pricked at each end with a pin, the white and yolk were carefully blown out and the shell kept in a box in cotton wool. We had eggs of the kingfisher, robin, jay, jackdaw, yellow linnet, to mention only a few, and each was labelled with its appropriate name. It was a most interesting hobby since the shapes and markings and colours of the eggs were specific to each bird.

Before leaving for school in the morning, Hal and I had certain chores to do about the farm after breakfast. At eight-fifteen we were mucking out the stables, fretting and rushing as we had a three-quarter-mile journey afterwards.

"Come on, hurry up, fetch the barrow and stop messing about," yelled Hal.

"I'm coming as fast as I can," I shouted, pushing a big, heavy wooden wheelbarrow almost as big as myself. "Move over, Bonny, move over-Bright," I said to the two cart-horses tied up in the stable.

The manure and straw loaded on to the barrow was too heavy for my puny arms to lift, so off would go my brother to the dung heap with it.

Then there was a frantic rush to change our jackets and boots and make our way to school. Hal had rigged up a bike and, with me as a passenger, we sped off at what seemed to me to be a dangerously high speed. We were not the only boys who had to earn their keep, but Cloggy Morgan came to school with his black boots covered with mud. He was a red-faced, gauche lad who found school a bore and was a true clod-hopper.

On our way home we passed a small wood which was dark and thickly populated with trees. I remember the Wills brothers chasing one of the village girls into this wood. There followed screams of protest from the girl and then all was silent. Some few minutes later they appeared, Maggy looking a little shame-faced and bewildered, and the Wills brothers rather triumphant. I wasn't particularly interested in these capers and didn't really understand what was going on.

The women who lived in the nearby houses understood, though, and were thoroughly outraged by this deplorable behaviour from the local young generation. Said one, "It's disgusting, it should be stopped."

"Yes," said another. "The wood ought to be cut down."

"I've a good mind to have Mr Rod watch the place," said the first.

Why Mr Rod, the local policeman, should spend his time in the wood to watch the kids coming home from school I couldn't imagine. Perhaps he would stand like a statue behind a trunk to catch these errant youngsters in their acts of depravity and, having observed these acts with his own eyes, step out and say in a stern, unrelenting voice, "You can't do that there 'ere." And that would be the end of the matter.

I think the wood was eventually cut down but for a different reason than that of improving children's morals.

In the small hamlet near the wood lived the church organist. He was always well turned out, with his bow tie and pinstriped suit, and was the local expression of sartorial elegance. Since he didn't appear to do any other kind of work, I often wondered how he managed to look so elegant on the pay of a parish organist.

I learned years later that he used to supplement his stipend by making and selling a cosmetic product. This was rouge, and the raw materials for his concoction were quite cheap. It consisted of bricks finely ground to a powder with a little perfume added!

★ ★ ★

Just after my eleventh birthday Hal reached the age of fourteen and left this seat of learning to take up farming. For quite long periods during the year he went to my grandfather's farm to gain additional experience. We had been very close as brothers, despite our many fights, and when he first left home I was terribly lonely.

It was about three months later that I went on to my seat of learning number three.

CHAPTER
FOURTEEN

Seats of Learning — Three

A headmaster who was prone to alcoholism and teachers who were not qualified produced a set of circumstances which was not conducive to learning. My parents and my paternal grandmother, who was a stickler for good education, noticed the lack of progress which I was making and decided that it was time that something was done about it. My father wrote to the chief education officer for the county and requested that I be transferred to a school for boys in Abergavenny.

The headmaster was a friend of the family, the discipline was strict and the standard of teaching was high. I was to sit the scholarship examination for the local grammar school in a year's time and I had a lot of leeway to make up. After three gruelling months I was promoted to the scholarship class, which was tutored by a master who had suffered severe shell-shock during the World War.

The effect of this was transmitted in no uncertain manner to the boys in his class. My six months there was sheer purgatory, for whilst the standard of teaching was high, we lived in terror of making the slightest mistake in our work, since retribution in the form of corporal punishment was swift and sure.

My uprooting from the easy-going country school and from my country companions, whom I understood and with whom I had so much in common, was like a shock to a tender plant which had not been sufficiently hardened off.

The town boys spoke a different language and were much more slick in their ways, which made me feel something of a country bumpkin. Life was tough but I learnt quickly both how to come to terms with my fellow pupils and how to cope with my lessons.

Our class master would screw up his eyes and squint along his cane as if he was taking aim with a rifle. When he had drawn a bead on the offending boy, he would rave like a demon possessed and order him to the front of the class. The outburst of frenzy would inevitably end with a few hard cracks of the cane.

However, he did not always have things his way. On one or two occasions the tougher lads rebelled and one day one of them scored a direct hit with a full ink-well. The silence was so intense that it could have been cut with a knife. Everyone fully expected that a full-blooded massacre would now follow. However, the boy was sent to the headmaster and nothing more was heard of the incident.

Most schools have their bullies and this one was no exception. There was one boy who decided that I was a tenderfoot and a suitable subject upon which to vent his hostility. By nature I was a passive sort of boy and not easily roused to anger, but this treatment began to assume proportions which were more than flesh and blood could stand. The German strategist, Clausewitz, in his book *The Principles of War*, put forward the element of surprise as one of the principles. I implemented this with devastating effect with this particular bully.

He was about to start his ear-twisting exercise when my fist, starting from knee height, caught him on the jaw with a fast-moving uppercut and laid him flat on the ground. He gazed up at me with a look of amazement and disbelief that such a thing could have happened to him. As with most bullies, he kept out of the way after this and I was looked on with more respect and regarded as being a bit of a dark horse.

Whilst I revelled in intelligence tests, I found arithmetical problems very trying and I used to grapple with these with a sense of frustration. I couldn't see any sense in many of them and neither could I see what use they would be to me in the future. For instance, who in their right mind would try to fill a bath with the plug out? Yet a question asked how long it took to fill a bath if the cold tap was flowing at such and such a rate, the hot tap at a different rate and the water flowed away at yet another rate. I would dearly have loved to have given the people who thought up this nonsense a piece of my mind.

163

My father had had the benefit of a grammar school education and could still recall smatterings of French and Latin but his arithmetic was of the type which could deal with farm accounts and not bath water.

He and William, the casual worker, used to sit night after night in the farm kitchen racking their brains to help me with my problems. William sat on the wooden settle, which, with its high back and sides, made an ideal draught excluder. The oil-lamp spread a warm light on the table and cast dark shadows in the far corners of the room. A big fire blazed in the grate and in its warmth stretched the Welsh collie, fast asleep after his day's work on the farm.

All was silent except for the ticking of the old grandfather clock and the occasional hiss of water and ligneous fluids which oozed out of the blocks of wood burning on the fire. My poor beleaguered brain could stand it no longer. With a near hysterical cry of despair I shouted, "It's useless to try any more, I'll never understand this."

Tears of frustration were welling up in my eyes as I spoke. My father was somewhat nonplussed by this outburst. William sat quite calmly, stroking his walrus moustache as his grey eyes studied me reflectively.

"Now, now, calm down, young man. You won't get anywhere if you get worked up into a state like this."

A wise old bird was William; a man of the world and, in his subtle way, a practical psychologist. His imperturbability was transmitted to me and once again we settled down to the problem before us. Meanwhile

William's grey matter had been busy and he came up with the solution.

"Ah! yes, it's really simple when you know how," I said, but such confidence soon faded away when the next problem was looked at.

The weeks were slipping by towards that fateful day in March when the examination was to be attempted. Meanwhile, a personal vendetta had developed between myself and this confounded arithmetic.

"I WILL master it, I WILL master it, I WILL pass this exam," I repeated over and over to myself so often that the auto-suggestion began to allay my fears.

The day of decision was at hand and, putting on a brave face, I set off for the bus with the parting words to my parents, "Don't worry, it will be all right."

I arrived at the local grammar school, where groups of other pale-faced, anxious-looking boys had come together from all parts of the surrounding countryside to enter this fierce competition which would affect their future careers.

It is always nice to look at an examination paper and recognise something that one can do. It instils confidence from the start. The day's ordeal over, we returned to our homes with the feeling that a great burden had been lifted from our shoulders.

One afternoon a week our class went to a handicraft school to learn the rudiments of carpentry. This made a welcome respite from our tyrannical master, besides providing an interesting hobby. The instructor was a likeable, easy-going man who did not insist on a rigid discipline. We chattered as we sawed, planed, hammered and sandpapered. Like one of the seven dwarves, I whistled as I worked. Our instructor walked casually up to me.

"Can I see your tongue?" he asked.

"Yes, sir," I said, poking it out.

He placed his finger on it and a moment later I had a strong taste of oil.

"That should stop the squeak," he said, and strolled off to see how the other boys were making out with their efforts.

At first I felt resentment at this treatment, then looked rather sheepish and finally saw the funny side of it. This was discipline of a different kind, nothing brutal about it and no bitter enmities aroused. Henceforth I confined my whistling to more suitable places.

One summer's morning the headmaster announced that he had the results of the scholarship examination. There was a tense hush as he began to read out the names of those who had obtained scholarships and places at King Henry VIII School, Abergavenny. As each name was read out, there was a loud cheer. Boys in school need only the slightest excuse to yell at the top of their voices and this provided a legitimate excuse.

When my name was called as having won a scholarship, the anticlimax was so great that I almost fainted on the spot and the hearty back-slapping nearly beat me into the ground. I thought that my ears were playing tricks on me and it took some moments for the wonderful truth to sink in. The first terrifying hurdle was over and the way was clear for me to attend my father's old school the following September. My desk mate, who had also attempted the examination, had failed to get a place and I could not help feeling compassion for him despite my own elation.

All the past few months of terror, tyranny and frustration were now proved to have been worth it and I felt as if I had been through a baptism of fire. By now I had moved into the top class of the school, where we had a master who really understood boys and who rarely had to resort to the use of the cane to maintain discipline. The occasional use of this instrument of punishment was reserved for the toughest cases where no amount of reasoning was effective.

We had been introduced to elementary science and the demonstrations for the preparations of hydrogen and oxygen had whetted my appetite to want to learn more of the mysteries of the world in which we lived. Some old textbooks of my father's were lying around the house and the ones on chemistry were of particular interest to me. I used to pore over these and wished that I had the means to carry out the experiments listed. This early interest was to grow and shape my future life.

With the burden of the examination lifted, the summer term was a carefree and happy one. Once again there was time to stand and stare, and cricket in the evenings, with no nagging thoughts that I should be studying.

During this summer there was a school outing to Wookey Hole caves in Somerset. All the boys and staff boarded the express train at Abergavenny in great excitement. There was a relaxed feeling between masters and boys as we sped on our way.

"My dad said we will go through the Severn Tunnel."

"Cor! Do we?"

"Yes, and he says it's five miles long and it only takes seven minutes."

"Golly! That's fast, isn't it?"

Suddenly the sun's light disappeared and sulphurous fumes and smoke seeped in through the windows.

"Shut the windows, I'm getting plastered with soot."

There was a mad scramble for the windows.

"Pull the thing up, stupid."

"I'm trying to."

"Oh! Gerrout of the way, you're hopeless."

At last the windows were shut and we sat in the dim light of the small electric bulbs, watching the dark sides of the tunnel flash past and anxiously wondering if the whole thing would collapse before we were through it. How terrible if the waters of the Bristol Channel came pouring down on us! Well, we had never been through the Severn Tunnel before.

Eventually, after a coach journey, we arrived at Wookey Hole. I well remember the massive stalactites and stalagmites and the constant drip, drip of salt-laden water which, over countless years, had built up these amazing pillars. We traipsed through the Witch's Cauldron and entered the large cave through which flowed the river Axe on its subterranean journey.

The river was ominously dark at the far corner of the cave. I seem to remember being told that, although it appeared to be quite still, it was moving at the rate of twelve miles an hour. There was a boat on the river, though how anyone would have the nerve to venture a trip in it I couldn't imagine. It seemed as though the river must flow to the very bowels of the earth and quench the fires of Hades.

Eventually we boarded the coaches and then the train for home. We arrived at our local station at eleven o'clock that night and I was met by my father. Walking home with him that night, we had to negotiate a bridge which had almost been washed away a couple of weeks previously by a terrific storm which had swept the eastern half of the county, turning small brooks into torrential rivers which uprooted trees and caused great devastation in the area.

The end of term at this school finally arrived. Whilst I was there, the school and I had a love-hate relationship, but now that the time had come to sever myself from it I could not help feeling a twinge of regret. Most of the boys I was leaving behind, but a few were to be my new form mates at the grammar school.

The summer vacation now stretched over a period of six weeks. What bliss!

During early September Sir Alan Cobham's Air Circus was to come to Abergavenny to give a display of aerobatics and trips for the public. The local newspaper was offering a free flight to ten of its regular readers, who were invited to fill up a form and the lucky ones would be drawn out of a hat.

This was the first time I had ever bought a newspaper and I filled in the form with my tongue in my cheek. Imagine my surprise when a letter arrived to say that I had won a ticket!

We saw very few aeroplanes in this part of the country, so when they began droning in like super-hornets to land in the flat field on the banks of the river Usk, it caused quite a commotion amongst the local inhabitants.

I was staying with some close friends of the family in town, as we called Abergavenny. They had a daughter near my own age whom I got on with very well. On the Saturday of the air display the weather was delightful, the hot September sun glaring down from a beautiful blue sky, and flying conditions were perfect. There was an assortment of planes; Tiger Moths, monoplanes and a couple of bi-plane passenger craft.

Gaily coloured refreshment stalls dotted the field and from the crystal waters of the Usk the occasional salmon heaved its bulk in pursuit of an unsuspecting fly. A backcloth of trees and mountains completed the picture.

At last the great moment arrived. At twelve years of age this was the great experience. In company with my girl friend, her small brother, their mother and Hal, who had come along to join in the fun, we entered the aircraft and took our places in the armchair seats. With a deafening roar the engines sprang into life, a bit of revving up and we were off, taxiing across the grass with ever-increasing speed. Suddenly the bumping stopped and we were defying the forces of gravity. Tension began to fade and we sat back to enjoy the fifteen-minute flight over the surrounding countryside.

"Ooh! Look at the river, it looks like a big snake."

"Doesn't the Little Skirrid look flat on top! I always thought it was more pointed."

We were passing over the cemetery when my girl friend's mother exclaimed, "What a lovely view of the cemetery."

I didn't think that this was an appropriate time to make this remark and fervently hoped that we wouldn't end up there as a result of an engine failure.

After a safe landing I thought that there was nothing in flying and would cheerfully go through the ordeal again.

By now the long holiday was drawing to a close and I began to make preparations for going to the next seat of learning.

CHAPTER
FIFTEEN

The Hereford Bull

For as long as I can remember, my grandfather kept a bull. It was a pedigree Hereford and was registered with the Hereford Herd Society, of which Grandpa was a member.

Herefords are most attractive, and were known in the district as the "white faced 'uns". Brown coats with white faces and briskets and pointed horns are characteristic of this breed, renowned in this country and the Americas for the excellent beef they supplied.

My uncle, who married my mother's sister, kept a pedigree Hereford bull and bred pedigrees. One of his bulls, called Trothy Hero, was exported to South Africa and became one of the prime founders of the Hereford herd in that country.

Of the cattle which my grandfather kept, about eight cows were kept for milking. The rest of the cattle roamed free in the remoter pastures of the farm and were much wilder as they were less accustomed to coming into contact with human beings. The milking cows, on the other hand, were almost domestic pets and all responded to names such as Curly, Daisy, Fanny, Brownie and Gertrude. Sad to relate, however, they finally ended up on someone's table, for such is the callousness of commerce.

The young bull calves, except the true pedigrees, were castrated, an operation which provided delicacies for the table, and the young bullocks were raised for two to three years for beef.

Amongst all these cattle the bull held pride of place. He was the sheik of the harem but, poor fellow, was not allowed the freedom he would no doubt have desired. He was not allowed to roam the green pastures with his many wives but was shut up in a shed and tied by a chain around his neck to a heavy, stout manger. Beyond the manger was a narrow passage from which he could be fed.

However he was a valuable animal and, as such, was well looked after. His food was the best, including fresh clover in the summer, but not too much at a time or this induced a condition known as "red water". What the precise biological effect was I don't know, but I remember when I was staying with my grandfather one summer that the bull's urine turned red and great anxiety was felt for his health. Rationing of the clover, however, appeared to clear up the condition.

He was also fed a rich mixture of freshly pulped swedes and turnips with ground corn and, as a special treat once a day, a small quantity of molasses was incorporated. William — for all the bulls bore this name — ate this with relish. I gathered that molasses was intended to maintain his virility as on occasions he had frequent calls for his services from neighbouring farmers' cows.

Whilst his shed was being cleaned out each morning, he was given the freedom of the farmyard, whereby he could get necessary exercise. William would rush from his shed and buck and kick up his heels like a spring calf. He did not behave a bit like the responsible father of many children.

The Williams which my grandfather kept through the years varied a great deal in temperament. He usually kept a bull for three or four years. Longer than this was not practicable as there was a risk of inbreeding as his daughters approached maturity. The Williams also finished their careers on the dinner table but there were one or two exceptions. An exceptionally fine animal would be sold to a farmer in another area or overseas to continue his part in procreation.

One particular bull seemed to have a grudge against humanity and the world in general and often let his temper get the better of him. One day he slipped his chain, smashed the shed door to splinters and entered the yard. Not content with this, he charged the five-barred gate leading to the orchard and smashed that likewise.

My grandmother, aunt and maid heard the bellowing and splintering of wood and rushed out to the front lawn overlooking the yard to find the cause of the commotion. William was already in the orchard and his newly found freedom had gone to his head completely. The men were all away from the house in the fields haymaking and there was nothing three women could do to halt the trail of destruction.

"Just you keep out of way," said my grandmother to my aunt. "That beast is dangerous. I've told your father time and time again that he should get rid of him. He'll be the death of somebody."

Then turning to the maid she said, "Go and fetch the men, there's no telling what the brute will do."

The bull had halted his marauding foray into the orchard to take a few bites of fresh grass.

The uneasy peace was soon shattered. The bull bellowed and made a headlong charge at Kitty, the pony, who had been watching this ferocious intruder very warily. In the nick of time she took evasive action and the wicked pointed horns of the enraged bull just missed her ribs as he tossed his massive head.

The old sow was wallowing in a bath of black mud and generally minding her own business. But not for long. The bull next directed his attention to her, pawing the ground and bellowing ominously. The sow, with a squelching noise as the sucking mud released her coated body, started out of her reverie and rushed off to the far corner of the orchard, grunting and snorting, partly with fear and partly at being disturbed at her ecstatic wallowing.

"He's a devil," said my aunt, for Kitty was her own pony. "I hope the men get here soon. I dread to think of the damage he'll do if he stays out much longer."

The bull, bent on mischief, rolled his eyes and continued pawing the ground and bellowing.

"Heaven forbid!" shouted my grandmother, as he turned his attention to the cluster of beehives against the tall holly hedge at the far side of the orchard.

The bull stalked up to the hives and inspected them for a moment or two whilst the bees buzzed angrily around his head. Whether or not a bee stung his nose is not known but, suddenly, he went berserk and hives began to topple one after the other.

"Oh! the wretch! There goes all that lovely honey and we were just about to take it out," cried my grandmother.

Thousands of bees formed a cloud more angry than any thunder cloud and the furious buzzing and stinging attacks enraged the bull even further. But the massed attacks of thousands repelled the huge beast, which roared off to find further mischief to do.

Fortunately the three men arrived from the fields and, armed with pikes and pitchforks, they set about the task of getting mad William back into his cell. Whether he had had enough from the bees and didn't fancy facing three determined men with pitchforks, I don't know, but he was finally induced, albeit grudgingly, to go back to his shed. The three toreadors then made sure that their bull didn't escape again.

There was little that could be done about the apiary which was not established again. This bull was soon sent to the slaughter house for he was becoming too dangerous to manage.

When I was staying with my grandparents during school holidays, it often happened that farmers from surrounding farms brought their cows to be serviced by the bull. Whenever a cow arrived in the farmyard I was instantly called into the house on some pretext or

176

other. My aunt or grandmother would appear from nowhere and call to me.

"Tom, I want you a moment. It's not safe for you to be in the yard when the bull is out," or "Will you chop me some wood for the fire? I need some quickly."

I obeyed the calls with a deep feeling of frustration. Having been brought up on a farm and having seen lambs and calves being born, the process of procreation in animals was accepted as a perfectly normal one. This was sex education at first hand, with no thoughts of a vulgar nature entering my mind.

I had seen the mating of poultry and of a ram with a ewe. In fact I had been with my father when he had spread a red pigment called raddle on the belly of the ram before letting him run with the ewes during the mating season. The raddle was used as an indicator, for when the ram served the ewe the pigment was transferred to the hindquarters of the ewe, thus indicating which ones had been served and also the approximate date on which this had occurred. The farmer could then calculate the lambing times to close dates and this enabled him to give assistance where necessary during lambing.

However, we did not keep a bull on our farm and I had not seen the mating act between a bull and a cow; hence the feeling of frustration at being kept out of the way. The very fact that I was called away from the scene made my curiosity even stronger, so I resolved to find a way to observe without being seen.

Buildings stood on two sides of the rectangular enclosed yard and the hay lofts above the sheds commanded a view of the yard. Accordingly, the next time I saw a cow being driven down the road towards the farm I disappeared into one of the lofts. It was customary to bring another cow along for company. This seemed to have a calming effect on the one which was to be served. I don't know what cows say to one another on such occasions but it seemed to me to be analogous to one taking a friend on a visit to the dentist to give one Dutch courage.

The arrival of the cows seemed to arouse immediately my grandmother's Victorian instinct of what was decent and I heard my name being called, firstly in a casual way and then more urgently when I did not appear.

"Drat it! Where is that boy? Have you seen him?" she called to Grandpa, who had no objection to my being present and with whom I had a strong understanding.

"I dare say he's gone down to the brook to do a bit of fishing," he replied.

She went off uneasily into the house, for she didn't want to be present in front of the other men when the act took place. This would be much too embarrassing!

I had my eye glued to a knot-hole in the loft door and stood there waiting with baited breath for the bull to be let out. I had a good view of the yard except for one corner by the coach house.

"I hope they don't get around there," I muttered to myself, "or I'll miss the whole thing."

The bull came out of his shed, raised his head and sniffed the air. His mate for the morning was a young heifer about to undergo the experience for the first time. She looked nervous and her tail was clamped tightly down over her hind quarters. She wasn't going to lose her virginity in a hurry!

The bull took his time and proceeded to indulge in a spell of love-making. He sniffed the heifer, threw up his head and made blowing kind of noises whilst his upper lip curled upwards to his nose. The mating overture continued in front of the bored audience of the farmer and Grandpa, whilst I was fascinated by the performance.

"Come on, William, get on wi' it," said Grandpa impatiently.

But William wasn't to be hurried in his courtship. The heifer wasn't being very responsive and when William became more ardent in his approach she suddenly bolted straight over the muck-heap, scattering dung in William's face as he chased after her in hot pursuit. He wasn't going to lose his new bride if he could help it!

The heifer careered madly around the yard and disappeared out of view behind the coach house.

"Hang it!" I exclaimed. "I hope they move from there."

The sight of William's ton weight made her shift rapidly into view again and still the chase went on.

"Stand still," shouted her owner as he ushered her into a corner.

William wasn't going to let this opportunity slip, and heaving himself on to his hind legs he clamped his forelegs on her back and completed the performance. The bull was then driven back into his shed, the farmer went his way with his cows, one of which was now the wiser for her new experience, and Grandpa went into the house to fill in the details in the Society's record book.

"Have you seen that boy?" asked Ggrandmother.

"No," replied my grandfather.

I waited until the coast was clear and made my way down the field to the brook, where I had laid some night-lines. No luck, however, no shining trout on the hook, but I made sure that my aunt and grandmother saw me returning from that direction later in the morning.

"Where have you been?" they asked.

"I've been to look at the fish-hooks," I replied truthfully.

Grandpa was very proud of his bulls. He paid many guineas for them and made sure that they had a good pedigree. He recouped his outlay by breeding good stock and selling pedigree bulls, and he was also able to charge a higher fee for the bull's services than was customary for a bull of inferior breed. He entered his bulls for the agricultural shows in the area and the bull shed was decorated with cards and silk rosettes as evidence of his success.

For weeks before, elaborate preparations were made. The bull's diet was carefully controlled and he was bathed two or three times a week. For this operation he was tethered by a rope passed through a ring in his nose to a post near the water tank in the yard. Buckets of warm water were brought from the copper at the house and poured over him. Handsful of soft soap from a large tin of the stuff, specially bought for the purpose, were rubbed into his coat and worked up into a lather. William took on a different appearance.

I was allowed to assist in this bathing, provided I kept clear of those deadly horns. After a thorough massage he was swilled down with buckets of water to rinse away all traces of soap. His coat was then brushed and combed until it gleamed and took on quite a curly appearance. What a picture he looked! Face and brisket white as the driven snow and reddish-brown hide sparklingly clean!

Throughout the washing William had remained as docile as a lamb and it was evident from his behaviour that he had enjoyed his bath. He was then led back into his shed, where a bed of clean straw had been put down for him.

A few more of these treatments and William would be ready for the show — but that is another story.

There was one bull of outstanding quality in every respect. His pedigree was first class, his fine physique and straight back won him many prizes and, for a bull, he had an exceptionally good nature.

The time was approaching when it would be necessary for him to go, and all at the farm were sorry to see this come to pass. At least there was the satisfaction of knowing that he was not destined for the butcher's shop since, as he was such a fine specimen, he had been booked for export to the Argentine at a price

181

of several hundred guineas — a lot of money in the early 1930s.

However, this was not to be. This William became ill a few weeks before he was due to leave. Everyone diagnosed the complaint as a "stoppage", a term which covered a multitude of things, including constipation. The veterinary surgeon prescribed certain medicines, which had no effect, so my grandfather resorted to an old remedy of boiled linseed. This was a slimy mess with a very characteristic odour and was forced down William's throat with a drenching horn. This was a cow's horn used to administer medicines to cattle and horses. The horn was filled with the medicine, the animal's mouth forced open and the liquid poured down its throat.

Despite regular dosing two or three times a day, there was no improvement in William's condition. The vet was baffled and was unable to make any diagnosis as to what was causing the trouble. The poor animal was obviously in pain and lay on the floor of his shed blowing hard.

Then one morning the farmhand went to see him and found him lying motionless on the floor of his shed. The prize bull was dead.

My grandparents were very upset by this tragedy, for the bull was not only docile but also a very valuable animal. His value was now but the few pounds which the knacker's yard was prepared to pay.

A further problem was met when it came to getting the bull out of the shed. He was a big animal, weighing around a ton, and it was not possible to drag him out of the shed, for he had swollen. The door had to be removed and part of the wall knocked down before this could be accomplished. This was no mean task either as the walls were almost three feet thick.

A post-mortem revealed the cause of his death. A small piece of baling wire, used to tie up the bales of straw at harvest time, had somehow found its way into his fodder. This was found in the bull's heart and had apparently worked its way from the stomach or intestines until it had arrived in this all-important organ. This was indeed a sad, unusual and unfitting end to such a fine animal.

However, the work of the farm must go on. There were calves to be fathered, more stock to be raised, and so the shed wall was rebuilt to make a home for the next pedigree William.

CHAPTER SIXTEEN

The Horse Show

The Abergavenny Horse Show was invariably held in early September. It was one of the big events of the year in Monmouthshire, for exhibitors came from far afield to show the produce of the farms, rose growers and other horticultural specialists to show their beautiful blooms, and manufacturers of farm machinery to exhibit the latest devices for easing the lot of the farmer.

Besides all the behind-the-scenes activity of the Show Committee, much planning and detailed preparation was going on at farms over a wide area. I had often heard about the Horse Show, as it was called, but I had never been to one.

One September I was staying with my grandparents and I was asked if I would like to go with them and my aunt and uncle. I needed no persuading, for had I not been helping to wash the bull regularly for the past couple of weeks in preparation for him to be entered?

My grandmother and aunt had also been making feverish preparations and when the day of the show arrived, bread, cake, butter and dressed poultry was ready to make its journey to the exhibitors' tents.

There was the usual early morning activity when the farm was to be left for a day. All the stock had to fed and attended to, the cows milked and so on, before breakfast was eaten. Then there was the mad rush to change into best clothes, with shoes shining like jewels, before we climbed into the trap to set off at a fast canter to meet the bus to take us the ten-mile journey to town.

When we arrived at the town park where the show was sited, a great bustle was apparent. Large vehicles carrying the show animals were queuing up to get into the park. We looked for the one bringing William the bull. He was in the care of my brother and Will the farmhand.

The sun shone from a cloudless sky and with approaching autumn there was a faint nip in the air. Tall elm trees stood on two sides of the park and a broad avenue of copper beech ran its length, connecting the two main entrances with the pairs of heavy wrought-iron gates. In the distance the bracken-covered mountains towered, majestic and silent, and looked down at the scurrying of the puny humans, aloof and unchanging.

"Come on, look lively," said Grandpa as we entered. He paid the five shillings entrance fee for Grandmother and myself and then added, "Let's go and see if William is here."

We were joined by my aunt, who had arrived earlier to put the produce in the exhibitors' tents.

"What are the entries like?" my grandmother asked her.

"Not bad at all. The poultry is good but I think we stand a fair chance of winning," she replied.

My grandmother and aunt had had many successes with their dressed poultry, for they had succeeded in breeding a strain of fowl which made a very good table bird that took some beating for fleshiness and tenderness.

"Come on," Grandpa said to me impatiently, eager to be off.

We made our way to the area where the animal pens were set up. What a sight those animals were! Huge shire horses, coats sleek and gleaming black, with pale blue and red silk ribbons tied into their carefully groomed manes. Their tails were tied up into neat bobs and the brass of the harness shone like burnished gold, whilst the leather had undoubtedly been polished with elbow grease. Their grooms walked them up and down while the judges watched every step with critical eyes.

"That's a good 'un," said Grandpa. "I'll put my money on that one," he added as he pointed out a fine horse. He knew his horseflesh so I just nodded agreement, not understanding the finer points of the judging.

In the sheep pens were the prize rams of different breeds with their thick fleeces; next to them were the sows and hogs. In another group of pens were the cattle — Shorthorns, Jerseys, Friesians and Herefords. All had their coats washed and groomed. It looked as though they were dressed in their Sunday best for the occasion.

"There they are," said Grandpa.

I looked in the direction in which his stick was pointing and saw Hal and Will giving William a last brush down before he was paraded in front of the judges. What a picture he looked! His noble head with white face and gleaming white brisket, his curly reddish brown coat and straight back, marked him out as a fine specimen of the Hereford breed.

"Did he behave on the journey?" asked Grandpa.

"Good as gold," said Hal. "Wasn't he?" he said, turning to Will for confirmation.

"Aye, that he was," agreed Will.

William was a very docile animal but they were taking no chances with him running amok. These were strange surroundings for him after his secluded existence back on the farm. He was tethered to a post by a stout rope through the ring in his nose. We had also brought a pole which would be attached to the ring to lead him around the show ring if he was lucky enough to win a prize.

"Let's go and have a look around while the judging is going on," said grandpa. "We'll see you two later on," he added to Hal and Will.

The park was filling up rapidly now as the sightseers began to arrive in their hundreds. Many came from the industrial areas of the hills and valleys. The sing-song Welsh accent of the miners and steel workers contrasted sharply with the brogue of the farmers from Herefordshire and Gloucestershire.

"Ooh! Look at that big bull," shrilled a sing-song voice.

"Dieu, he's well developed," sang her male companion and added a crude, unprintable comment on the bull's virility. The woman tittered shrilly and whispered something in his ear which made him throw back his head with raucous laughter.

"These daios bent got much sense of animals," rasped one old farmer who overheard the remarks. "I'll bet they would move sharpish if they were put in a field with him."

Grandpa and I made our way towards the farm implements. Every few yards he stopped to have a chat with old cronies whom he hadn't seen since last market day.

"Looks like being a good show this year, John."

Old John Jenkins stopped, leaned on his stick, took off his cap and scratched his bald head whilst he contemplated this observation. His eyes peered out from a deep red face as he looked around him. At last he seemed to have got the situation sized up.

"Aye, I reckon it won't be bad, it won't be bad," he replied.

The implements looked resplendent on the green turf. They were painted in brilliant reds and yellows. There were the latest models of reapers, hay-turners, ploughs — implements of every description. The farmers milled around examining them in every detail while the salesman stood by expectantly, awaiting orders.

"'ow much be this then?" asked one farmer and, when he was told the price, muttered in a hard-done-by tone, "I couldn't afford that sort of money," trying to create the impression that he was well-nigh penniless. Oh, a hard life, farming — money always going out, hardly any coming in!

We next passed a marquee from which came the sound of dogs barking. There were shrill yaps and deep-throated barks, soprano barks, alto barks and bass barks, neither in unison nor in harmony, but just an unorchestrated symphony of dog noises. We peeped through the flap of the tent, for the public were not allowed in until the judging had finished.

"By gum, there's some dogs!" murmured grandpa as we caught a glimpse of terriers, Pekinese, spaniels, labradors, retrievers and alsatians. "I wouldn't like that lot loose among the sheep."

By now we had come almost full circle and we had reached the tents where the produce was on show, but as the judging was in progress we couldn't go in. The time was now approaching mid-morning. The beer tent was open and Grandpa decided that it had been a thirsty business doing our tour of inspection, so he made a bee-line for the refreshing brew.

"What are you going to have?" he asked, diving his hand into his breeches pocket.

This sudden invitation made me feel quite manly and grown up, but I was rather at a loss for words to reply. I hesitated and then said, "I don't know. What are you having?"

"I'm going to have a spot of beer, but I can't get you that or I'll get into trouble. How about a lemonade?"

I settled for that. When I had drank a little, Grandpa furtively tipped a drop of his beer into my glass to give it a bit of flavour, as he said. We stood outside the tent, Grandpa sipping his beer and I getting more blown up every moment on my beer-flavoured fizzy lemonade.

I stood around for a time while Grandpa chatted to a few of his friends over a couple of pints. Suddenly he put down his, now empty, glass, picked up his stick and said, "I'll warrant they've finished the judging now. Let's go and see how William has fared."

We went off to the stock pens and straight to the Herefords. There stood Hal and Will with broad beams on their faces, whilst William now wore a red rosette and had won yet another trophy for the bull-cot. He hadn't let his predecessors down!

"Well, what do you think of that, boss?" asked Will, pointing proudly to the red silk.

"I knew he had a good chance," replied Grandpa, a pleased smile creasing his leathery face. "Good old William," he said, patting his neck affectionately.

"Baw," said William, rolling his eyes and gently shaking his head to and fro.

Some of the other bulls were blowing and pawing the ground with their hooves and didn't look at all happy at the way things were. Professional jealousy, no doubt!

"Now then, you two," said Grandpa, turning to Hal and Will. "You'd best go and get yourselves something to eat and drink. We'll stay here with William until you get back. And you had better have a look around when you're at it."

Off they went, glad to be free of their responsibilities for a while.

"This has made my day, Tom," said Grandpa, and added, "I wonder how the womenfolk have got on. If they have done as well as we have, they won't have much to grumble about."

At that moment he glanced across to where the shire horses were standing.

"There, what did I tell you?" he exclaimed, pointing with his stick at a big black horse. "That's the one I told you would win."

Sure enough, it had won first prize and I was more than ever convinced that Grandpa knew his horseflesh.

The time passed quickly and my brother and Will soon appeared to take charge again. William would soon go into the grand parade around the ring with all the other animals, and Hal had the job of leading him around it with the prizewinners in single file.

As there was an hour or so before the grand parade, we filled in the time by visiting the flower and produce tents. The roses were magnificent. Beautiful, perfectly formed blooms were on display and many of the latest varieties were being shown. Grandpa was quite a rose fancier and propagated roses by budding on to briars which he dug out of the hedgerows. It was not much wonder, then, that such beauty should attract his immediate attention.

"By gum, there's some fine roses," he said, his voice full of appreciation, as we made our way over to the stands to have a closer look.

He was peering closely at them and smelling the rich blooms. After a while, when he had examined each one, he went over to one of the people on the stand and was soon in close conversation with him. After a few minutes of animated discussion I saw the salesman write something on a pad of paper. He tore a sheet off and handed it to Grandpa, who folded it carefully and put it in his pocket. A quicker look at the other flowers, and off we went into the produce marquee.

This was milling with people. We looked at the sea of faces and presently spotted those of my grandmother and aunt. When we got nearer I could see a rosy flush on my aunt's high cheekbones and she looked quite excited.

"You're looking mighty pleased with yourself," said Grandpa.

"And so I should," she replied, chuckling. "After all, we got a first for poultry, butter and cake."

"Did you be blowed!" exclaimed grandpa. "Well, I didn't do badly either. William pulled off a prize too."

"You don't say!" gasped Grandmother.

"What's so surprising about that? He's a good 'un, is William."

"Have you been to see the flowers yet?" queried my aunt.

"Yes," I replied. "We've just come from there."

"Oh yes," said Grandpa, "I've bought a rose bush. They'll send it on in the late autumn."

"Which one did you order?" asked Grandmother.

"Bother me, I can't remember the name but it's a beauty. Just wait a minute, I've got it here."

He fished out the sheet of folded paper and handed it to my grandmother. She studied the writing through her spectacles.

"Madam Butterfly, I remember that one," she said. "You made a good choice," she added approvingly.

The time was now approaching for the Grand Parade and already people were taking up vantage points close to the ring. We hurried over to William to see if Hal and Will had everything under control. They were ready to go, William had the pole fixed to the ring in his nose and Hal looked very smart in his white coat.

"Here, take this," he said, handing me his Kodak Brownie. "Try and get a snap of us going around the ring."

I took the camera and rushed off to find a good spot from which to take the photographs. I had just found one when I heard my name called. I turned to find myself gazing into the eyes of the daughter of a friend of the family. They were twinkling with a "come-and-join-me" look. We needed no introduction and so we spent the remainder of the day together.

By now the crowds were pressing several deep against the sturdy rail of the ring. Fortunately we were in the front and had an uninterrupted view of the parade. The incessant chatter of the crowd paused for a moment and then up went the shout, "Here they come."

The proud winners were filing into the ring from the direction of the animal pens. I quickly removed the box camera from its brown canvas bag and sighted it in the direction of the approaching animals with their wards.

The gleaming, proud-stepping shire horses came and went. The sheep, cows and heifers led by their halters were followed by the bulls. Hal was coming along quite well leading William, who was still well behaved and docile.

Click, went the camera.

"Did you get them all right?" asked Muriel.

"I hope so. I hope it comes out all right," I replied.

"Well, they come round again, so you can have another try," she reminded me.

On the second time around they filed out to return to the pens and once more the ring was empty.

But not for long. Into the ring came the high-stepping trotters drawing light two-wheeled carriages. The grace of these horses was something at which to marvel. It seemed that their forelegs would bump their proud muzzles, they lifted them so high. This was a long-awaited competition and the judges were watching the competitors with critical eyes. I didn't fully appreciate the artistry of the performers but it was very pleasing to watch. No doubt if Grandpa had been with me he would have explained the finer points. When the winner had been decided he did a few rounds of the ring to the enthusiastic applause of the bystanders.

The entertainment which followed was competitive show jumping. This created a considerable amount of interest and, as the riders approached the more difficult jumps, it seemed as if the whole crowd held their breath.

"Gosh! I thought he would never clear that jump," gasped Muriel, gripping my arm in her excitement.

Feeling her hand on me like this set me wishing that all the jumps were as difficult or, indeed, even more difficult.

With so many interesting things to look at, the afternoon had passed quickly to early evening. The show was about to draw to a close with the final rousing event of the day.

Suddenly the Monmouthshire Hunt burst into the ring, the hounds in full cry with the red-coated, black peak-capped huntsmen galloping round blowing a lively tantivy on the horn. Around and around the ring they sped to the full-throated applause of an appreciative audience.

The band struck up the National Anthem and the show was over for another year.

A hubbub from the animal pens drifted across the rapidly emptying park: engines of the transports revving and the shouts of men getting the animals into them. A scurry of people cleared the produce tents, taking away the winners' entries which they had purchased for their tables.

And now the park was empty except for the deserted tents. Pieces of paper fluttered across the trampled turf, and the mountains looked dark in the shadow of the sinking sun.

After the excitement of the day the small market town was left once again to its sleepy self.

CHAPTER
SEVENTEEN

Seats of Learning — Four

In the September of my twelfth year I entered my next seat of learning to undergo a grammar school education. The school was not a large one, having about one hundred and eighty boys between the ages of eleven and nineteen. It had been founded by King Henry VIII and had turned out future citizens of integrity, some of outstanding ability who eventually reached the heights of their chosen professions.

The attractive sandstone building stood in its own grounds and was surrounded by lawns, tennis courts, playgrounds and, later, a modern gymnasium containing changing rooms and shower baths under the same roof. When I joined the school, however, the gym was in the Great Hall and, before going in to prayers each morning, every boy was required to change into plimsolls.

For the first few days we juniors stood in awe of the masters in their gowns and mortar boards and felt that this was indeed a seat of learning and that we were now true budding academicians.

There was also the chemistry laboratory, the very smell of which filled me with delight and further awakened in me the urge to learn more of this fascinating subject. No spur was needed to make me attentive to my science studies but, strangely enough, the subject in which I excelled was Latin.

We had a young and enthusiastic Latin master whom we considered to be one of us. He was also a good sportsman, captained the local cricket team and played hockey for Wales, and this earned him further respect.

Our first step in Latin was to learn the feminine declension.

"We will decline *puella*," he said. "Repeat after me, *puella, puellam, puellae, puellae, puella* which is the singular declension for *puella*, meaning girl."

A wisp of a smile played around his lips as he said this, no doubt thinking that we would approve of the subject.

"In the plural we have *puellae, puellas, puellarum, puellis, puellis*. Now your prep tonight will be to learn this declension and I will test you tomorrow."

The next day's Latin period began.

"You, Evans, give me the ablative plural of *puella* and spell it."

Evans, looking a little embarrassed, got slowly to his feet, cleared his throat and said his piece.

"Police — p-o-l-i-c-e."

Gales of laughter echoed around the room. This didn't please our Latin guide and mentor in the slightest.

"You will stay for detention tonight."

197

When the period had finished, some half a dozen boys were booked for detention and this in itself proved to be a somewhat unconventional procedure.

Our Latin master had a habit of tugging his gown free whenever it got caught in a desk as he walked between the rows. The net result of this tugging was that, from the waist down, his gown hung in strips of about an inch or so in width. At the end of the strips were tied large knots.

Instead of being detained after school, the boys were lined up at the far side of the classroom and our master stood at the doorway, twirling one of the strips with the knot at the end.

"Right, run for it," he said with a broad grin.

Each boy in turn would make a mad dash for the door. If he wasn't lucky he went home rubbing his rump.

The school was providing us with new experiences, new problems and new fountains of knowledge. Budding scientists and budding linguists lumped together in the lower forms to obtain a general education in the arts and sciences before being allowed to develop their true aptitudes. As regards responsibilities, we were somewhat schizophrenic in behaviour.

On the one hand we were conscientious workers, but on the other hand we were continually carrying out the most atrocious japes — at least we thought they were, and, judging from the uproar they caused, I guess we weren't far wrong. There was a continual battle of wits between masters and boys. Some of these japes were quite ingenious and almost drove our poor French

198

master to the point of having a nervous breakdown. He, unfortunate fellow, was a poor disciplinarian but one of the kindest of men that one could meet. However, there was always the irresistible temptation to play him up. He tried to assert his authority by the use of a little sarcasm but this only earned him the nickname of "Sark". From the first day, each new form entering the school was indoctrinated with the peculiarities of each master, his strengths and his weaknesses.

On two occasions whilst I was at the school, we had fresh masters join the staff. These were soon put through our evaluation tests and, depending on their behaviour under our jape technique, were accepted or not accepted as sports. If he was accepted, then henceforth he had our full cooperation and was dubbed "one of the lads".

One afternoon Sark was due to take us in French. Elaborate preparations had been made for a jape. The reproduction pictures of the old masters, which were hung around the room to instil some appreciation of the arts into us, had been connected together with strong thread of the same colour as the walls. A further length of thread dangled down to the side of a desk.

When Sark entered all was quiet — ominously quiet; each boy was bending over his desk, apparently absorbed in his work. This was the lull before the storm and poor old Sark knew this, for a few minutes was usually necessary to restore order before the lessons could commence.

"Now let us get on. Lewis, start reading aloud paragraph two on page twenty-eight."

Lewis began to read French in his Monmouthshire brogue, which was a mixture of the Herefordshire and Welsh accents. Suddenly, as if moved by some mysterious force, the pictures began to sway gently, to and fro, to and fro. No-one appeared to take any notice of this phenomenon and all seemed to be absorbed in their work. Sark couldn't believe his eyes.

"Stop this nonsense," he said rather uncertainly.

There was complete silence whilst the pictures continued to sway.

"Stop this nonsense — at once," in a louder voice this time.

We looked up with blank expressions.

"We're not doing anything, sir."

"Not — not doing anything," he spluttered. "Stop moving those pictures."

"It's very strange, sir. How can we be moving them?"

Our hands were on our desks and no-one was moving, apart from the boy against the wall who was gently tugging the dangling thread.

It seemed that this was a complete mystery, and so it was until Sark, now almost at his wits' end, walked up to one of the pictures, peered at it closely through his specs and finally found the connecting thread. It didn't require very expert detective work to trace the cause of the disturbance to the offending miscreant, who was promptly banished to the corridor for the rest of the period. This was Sark's method of restoring order.

I must confess that my rather ebullient sense of humour resulted in my spending many of the French periods in the corridor during the couple of years immediately prior to the matriculation examination.

Our headmaster, whom we all liked, was known affectionately as "Neddy". No-one knew how he came by this name but he was a very efficient head and one of the youngest ever to be appointed at that time. One afternoon another fellow and I had been kicked out of French and were standing in the corridor near Neddy's study when he came out and saw us.

"Ah! so you have been tormenting Mr — again, have you? Come with me."

We entered his study and he took his cane off its hook on the wall and began to bend and swish it in a threatening manner.

"Hold out your hands. I'm not going to hurt you, it's the indignity of the punishment that matters."

We each received a couple of gentle taps. This had a greater effect than a thrashing, which would have aroused resentment. A mental hurt rather than a physical one was felt. To me he said, "Don't go into French periods for the rest of the session."

This was matriculation year, so I decided that I must concentrate my energies on Latin as it was imperative that I had a language in this all-important examination. Thus during French periods I found myself a quiet corner in the library and devoted all my energies to Latin syntax, Caesar's *Gallic War* and Virgil's *Aeneid*. As things turned out — and it was totally unexpected — I passed in French as well as Latin.

★ ★ ★

One summer's evening during my first year at the school a plague of may-bugs hit our part of the country. They came in dense swarms and the air was black with them. At times it was almost impossible to find anywhere there was not one of these large insects. I collected a number of them in a box and took them to school to learn French. The plan misfired a little as they were not so lively in broad daylight as they were at dusk. However, we managed to get a number airborne, much to the annoyance of Sark and the amusement of the boys.

Various other devices were used to arouse consternation in class. Some of these seemed to be strokes of genius at the time, but on reflection, now appear puerile — as I suppose they really were. Thus putting calcium carbide in the ink-wells to produce the unpleasant smell of impure acetylene was, in reality, more of a self-inflicted punishment than an amusing joke.

The school was heated by fires in each classroom and one day we thought a period in the fresh air would be preferable to staying indoors. This was arranged quite simply by stuffing a couple of dusters up the chimney in the period between lessons, and adding a little small coal to the fire. By the time the master walked in, smoke was rapidly filling the room. Amidst coughing and spluttering we were ordered out into the fresh air, the last boy hanging back to remove the dusters before they were discovered. We often wondered about the staff room conversations regarding these odd occurrences.

On one occasion I distributed tiny packets of sodium carbonate to each boy, with instructions to sniff a small pinch when the French lesson got under way. The result of this experiment was to induce a fit of genuine sneezing amongst all those who indulged. Sark couldn't understand why a class of thirty boys should suddenly begin to sneeze in concert. He undoubtedly realised that this was no coincidence, but as to the cause, that was a different matter.

Perhaps it was wrong of us to waste our time in this manner, but we did cram in a lot of work and these high-spirited pranks helped to keep a balance between sanity and insanity.

However, I felt that they could be carried too far. It was all right to balance a book or two over a doorway to catch the incoming master for the next period, but I thought that plastering the seat and top of the master's desk with treacle was overstepping the mark.

This prank misfired since the French period was replaced at the last moment by an English lesson. The substitute master didn't appreciate in any way that he couldn't move his book off the desk top, and even less the fact that the seat of his trousers was stuck to the seat of the desk. I can't remember what happened to the culprit but I'm sure that it wasn't a very pleasant experience.

Our form, over the first three years, had been getting the reputation of being the worst form as regards behaviour to enter the school in living memory. Perhaps this was said of every form, but we certainly had some good rugby players amongst us. What I did not know then was that a number of my fellow pupils were to perish in the war to come and some were to be decorated for gallantry.

To break the monotony of school life and to increase our knowledge of the Shakespearian theatre, we had an annual outing to Stratford-on-Avon. Lunch over, we trooped to the theatre for the afternoon performance. There was nothing so imposing as this edifice in Abergavenny, both in the fabric of the building itself and in its luxurious internal appointments.

During the interval we repaired to the gents, where one of the fellows encountered liquid soap for the first time.

"What's this stuff?" he asked.

"Oh! That's hair oil," we said, winking at one another.

"Gosh! That's good of them to provide that. I'm going to try some."

Whereupon he proceeded to plaster his hair with it. It was only then that he noticed that other more adult visitors were using the "hair oil" to wash their hands. In a panic he doused his hair with water to wash it off. His head was covered in a voluminous lather and he soon became the centre of interest. Perhaps people wondered why on earth it was so necessary for a seventeen-year-old youth to wash his hair during the interval of *Macbeth* in the Shakespeare Memorial Theatre at Stratford-on-Avon in the County of Warwickshire.

We left him wrestling with his coiffure and went back to our seats. Some while later he rejoined us, looking very embarrassed. Thereafter he was known as "Soapy".

One year we travelled to Stratford by coach instead of by train. After the theatre and a high tea at one of the restaurants, we were allowed to wander around the town and riverside walks to see the points of interest in the town. Strict instructions had been issued that all boys were to report to the coach at half past eight for the return journey.

At the appointed time all were assembled with the exception of four boys. Fifteen minutes later they had not turned up and Little Len, our English master, was becoming rather agitated.

"Where are those louts?" he asked, making no attempt to disguise his annoyance.

Everyone looked blank.

"We must organise a search at once," said Little Len. The boys split up, with instructions to search particular areas and report back every fifteen minutes. Eventually Little Len himself caught the four emerging from a pub in a very merry state. The riot act was read, with the stern promise that this unseemly behaviour would be reported to the Head next day, and the coach finally departed at nine-thirty.

On the following day the four miscreants were paraded before Neddy with Little Len's Lancashire voice intoning the indictment.

"These four louts delayed the coach by one hour and I eventually found them emerging from a cider house in a state of inebriation."

Neddy looked as severe as he could under the circumstances, but I can't remember any dire punishment being inflicted upon the four adventurers.

Up to the age of sixteen I had been a soccer fan and didn't understand rugby football, which was the only winter sport played at our school. My parents weren't keen for me to play the game as they considered it to be too rough and dangerous. I had a quiet word with my paternal grandmother, who was very go-ahead in most things, and she soon got the matter sorted out to my advantage. I became so engrossed with the game that I found myself playing for the first fifteen within a year. I realised what I had been missing and put everything into it. In the heat of battle all came equal to me, whether they were eight stones or fourteen. "The heavier they were, the heavier they fell" was my motto, and there was a certain amount of satisfaction in being able to tackle one's sports master and bring him crashing to the ground, knowing that this was all part of the game.

Whenever I think of those rugby days I have a feeling of nostalgia. There is a comradeship amongst rugby players and this lived on through my university days up to the present time. Although it is a tough and physical game, there has never been vandalism or fighting amongst the fans, as is found in today's football crowds. It is a man's game for men.

I can see thirty lusty fellows, stripped to their birthday suits, under the showers, washing away the mud, bruises and aches whilst the air was heavy with steam and the odour of sweaty togs and socks. All were singing heartily the songs of the day: "Does your mother come from Ireland", "Cowboy", "The chapel in the moonlight", "Who loves you?" and so on. There were also typical rugby songs, such as the one about four and twenty virgins who came down from Inverness to go to a ball.

When I was eighteen I had a dark, stiff beard and, to maintain an air of respectability, it had become necessary to shave twice a week. This operation I carried out, at no small hazard to myself, using my father's "cut-throat" razor. After some time I found the process of having to grow new flesh at such frequent intervals such a tedious one that I resorted to the use of a safety razor.

I usually shaved after a rugby match, rather than before, since my stubby beard proved a useful weapon in the scrum and my face did not suffer from soreness. One Wednesday afternoon we were in the showers after a match when one of the fellows said, "Hey, TC, I'll bet you that you won't shave for a week."

"How much?" I asked.

"A bob."

"Poof, that's not worth it," I replied, hoping to get the odds up.

"I'll add another sixpence to that," yelled two others.

"Done," I said. "I'll not shave for over a week."

I hadn't realised until the bet was concluded that this was a conspiracy. Each morning at prayers one of the prefects read the morning lesson from the big carved oak desk which had been dedicated to a former pupil who had reached the height of his academic profession at Oxford University. I was soon reminded that I was due to read the lesson, when my beard would be at its luxuriant best.

However, there was a principle at stake here, besides the one and sixpence, and I was determined to go through with it, come hell or high water. On the following week Thursday morning, as usual, I walked from the bus station through the main street to the school. The sight of a small cap perched above a bearded face evoked a fair quota of stares and smiles from the townsfolk but, undaunted yet feeling a complete idiot, I marched on.

After the hymn I walked from the back of the hall, past the line of masters, to the platform. The news of the wager had swiftly passed around the school and I suspect that the masters also knew of it. Our Latin master held his hymnbook in front of his face to conceal his mirth, others tried to look blank, and Neddy's eyes popped slightly as I arrived on the platform. Broad grins appeared on the boys' faces and subdued titters floated around the hall.

I used to go to the bank once a week for Neddy. When I went to him this particular day he looked hard at my cheeks and said, "You'll soon have to start shaving, won't you?"

"Yes, sir! I'm waiting until the weekend. We have a match on Saturday and playing in the scrum makes my face sore if I shave before."

"Ah yes, you must be careful not to do that."

I then went and collected my one and sixpence with a relatively clear conscience.

My fellow pupils and I were now becoming rapidly aware that girls were girls and that they were creatures which merited a deeper interest than we had taken in them heretofore. The local high school for girls had many white-bloused, black-gym-slipped, black-stockinged beauties who induced a strong rivalry amongst the fellows competing for their affections. In fact it seemed that the country was filled with girls galore.

There was one sixteen-year-old who lived near the school and whose gymslip didn't stretch far below her waist. She was regarded as having the finest pair of legs in the neighbourhood, and a short gymslip provided an excellent excuse to show them off. I think she also had a pretty face but our eyes rarely reached that kind of elevation.

One year, when I was in the fifth form, I was asked by Little Len, who taught English and history to the senior school, to take part in the annual debate. I forget what the motion was about, except that it was to do with the Colonies. The debate was to take place in the school hall and, as I later learned, there were to be further performances at the girls' school and also at a public hall in the town.

At first I refused to have anything to do with this since I didn't consider myself competent to deliver a speech in front of a critical audience, or even to write sufficient sense to compose a speech in the first place. Little Len tried every persuasion to make me change my mind and finally pleaded with me, although I can't think why.

"Oh! come on, TC, please, Tom, do say yes."

I almost felt as if I was being proposed to as he had never spoken to me like this before. I can only suppose he wanted me in the debate to have a contrast and to show how good the stars really were. Perhaps this was being unkind to him, but anyway, I accepted his kind invitation in the end.

When we were informed that the girls were holding a debate themselves on a similar subject, I quite innocently made a suggestion which was construed as being a wisecrack.

"If the girls are holding a similar debate, might it not be a good idea if we who are taking part went and listened to the girls' speeches?" I asked.

"Why?" asked Little Len. "Ah don't think it's necessary."

"But we might be able to pick up a bit of material," I retorted.

This was immediately taken in the worst possible sense by the boys, who roared with laughter. Little Len replied with a cold stare and I felt rather embarrassed since I hadn't intended the remark to have any double meaning.

I was of the opinion that a speech is much more interesting if some light relief is introduced here and there, and when I wrote my version a certain amount of humour was included. Little Len vetted all the speeches and when mine was returned it contained a number of blue-pencilled deletions. However, when the time came for it to be delivered I gave the unexpurgated version, with no disastrous consequences and no comment from Little Len.

The headmaster's son, whom I will call Hue, joined the school at the same time as I did, and we went right through the school together, becoming good companions as time went on. We were two of a kind, being a little on the wild side and always ready to try some kind of a lark. In retrospect some of our escapades were undoubtedly foolish.

When I was in the sixth form I had a free run of the chemical laboratory. During the time when I had no lessons to attend, I was experimenting and carrying out analytical techniques, for I had now decided that chemistry was to be my career.

One day Hue and I decided that we would try our hand at making gunpowder, which is an experiment many budding young scientists feel they must do. The ingredients were carefully mixed in their correct proportions. Having made something, it is a natural enough desire to want to see if it works. We couldn't very well make an explosion in the school grounds and we began to consider ways and means of testing our product. The simplest solution to our problem was to prove rather more effective than we had anticipated.

The room across the corridor from the laboratory was empty as the form were in the gym. A red, smokeless fire glowed in the grate. The gunpowder was

211

rammed into a test-tube and the tube tightly corked. We dropped the tube into the fire and popped smartly back into the lab. No sooner had we closed the lab door than there was a terrific bang. Windows rattled, doors shook, there was the clatter of racing feet in the corridor and it seemed as if all hell had been let loose.

Partly to see how our stuff had worked — as if we didn't know! — and partly to allay suspicion, we rushed in too. The fire had been blown out of the grate and the hot coals were beginning to scorch the wooden block floor. The fat, red-faced cleaning lady, Neddy, and several other masters and boys were already in action and, not to be outdone, Hue and I set to to help clear up the mess.

Neddy looked at us very suspiciously and said, "Do you know anything about this?"

"It must have been some explosive in the coal," I ventured, which was true but not a straight admission of guilt.

"Humph! Very dangerous," said Neddy, and walked off.

I fancy that he thought this explanation too simple but he said no more about it.

This episode and several others not so drastic must have ingrained me in his memory, for when, six years later, after the war, I wrote to him for a reference and asked him if he remembered who I was, he started his letter thus: *Dear TC, Can I ever forget you . . .*

But he gave me a very glowing reference!

★ ★ ★

My successful experiments with gunpowder enabled me to make fireworks. It also came in useful in another way. One summer we found a wasps' nest in the middle of one of the hay-fields, and this constituted a danger: if the horses were stung, a dangerous situation could arise. We usually got rid of wasps' nests by pouring a solution of sodium cyanide down the hole. I thought it would be interesting to try and blow out the nest with some of the gunpowder. One evening, when the inmates had retired for the night, I rammed a quantity down the hole, fixed a fuse and lit it. There was a roar, and smoke and flames belched from the hole. I dug out the nest with a spade and took the combs to school for the biology master.

"Thank you, TC," he said. "Put them in a drawer in the lab, please."

Three days later, when he had decided to use the combs in a lesson, he opened the drawer and a cloud of wasps flew out, much to the consternation of master and pupils.

To travel to school I had about a fifty-minute journey. It was always a rush to catch the train or bus as I was very tardy in leaving my bed in the morning. When I was travelling by train, the routine was invariably the same. I would rush downstairs, grab a piece of bread and butter and a cup of cocoa, snatch up my bag of books and rush out of the door straight on to my bike, which my father would be holding ready like some patient horse.

I had about a mile to go to the station and often the train was signalled before I left the house. Then there would be a mad dash along the narrow twisting road. In order to cut out a steep hill and shorten the distance, I often followed a private drive through the farmyard of a market gardener. This drive, after passing through the farm buildings, continued alongside the railway line and then parallel to the station platform.

Many times I jumped off my bike, climbed over the fence and sprinted up the side of the line on to the platform with the waiting train, the guard with his flag poised to wave and the porter with his hand on the door handle. I gasped my thanks between gulps of air and we were on our way. The kind porter would then stroll round and collect my transport and leave it at the local pub for my collection in the evening. This voluntary task probably provided him with relaxation after these regular morning crises. I don't know if the station staff ran a book on whether I would make it in time each day!

When I was travelling by bus, I and a small group of other country boys arrived at the school before the doors were open. Purely by chance, I found that a key which I had obtained at a sixpenny store fitted the lock of the back door. We were then able to let ourselves in and save ourselves the tedium of waiting until Neddy arrived with the front door key to open up the school. This system worked fine until some of the boys got into the habit of waiting at the front door whilst I opened up for them. I thought that I had encouraged this laziness far too long, so one morning I let myself and one or two others in through the back door and decided to leave the front door locked. Those waiting at the front began to ring the bell and hammer on the door with shouts of, "Let us in. Let us in."

I ignored their pleas and for a while all was quiet. Then the ringing and knocking started again.

"Don't be so damned lazy," I shouted. "Walk round to the back like the rest of us."

Then followed some rather uncomplimentary remarks from my end. In the brief interval of silence that followed I heard Neddy's voice.

"What's the matter with the fellow, is he insane?"

Without more ado I opened the door and Neddy swept in.

"Good morning, TC," he said, carrying on to his study.

"Good morning, sir," I replied, feeling a complete idiot.

That was the one morning when he had forgotten his key.

One Christmas holiday I had been staying at my grandparents' farm. I had taken a twelve-bore double-barrelled shotgun and my ferret for a few days' shooting, and when I returned home it was not convenient to take the gun or the ferret with me. My brother, who was at my grandfather's at that time, brought them into town on market day and I collected them from him during the lunch hour and took them back to school with me in the afternoon.

Our first lesson was mathematics. By my desk was the gun and the ferret, neither of which had been noticed by our maths master. Nelson, the ferret, was in a wooden box with a piece of perforated zinc over the top to admit air. He became restless and began to scratch the lid of the box.

"Stop fidgeting and get on with your work," said our master.

He was a good sporting type who also came from a farming family so, after a few remarks of this sort, I thought it best to do a bit of explaining. He was very charming about it, had a look at Nelson and the lesson continued without any more fuss.

The last lesson of the afternoon was French and we thought that we would have some fun with Nelson and Sark. Nelson by now had gone to sleep so, to rouse him, we sprinkled a few crumbs on to the zinc grating. At the smell of food Nelson became very active and began scratching in earnest.

"Be quiet," shouted Sark, and not a muscle moved.

Sark was now as non-plussed as when he encountered the episode of the pictures three years ago.

"Be quiet," shouted Sark again and still not a muscle moved.

By now I was beginning to feel rather sorry for him.

"It's my ferret, sir," I said.

"Your what?"

"It's my ferret," I said, and went on to explain, "He's getting restless cooped up in a small box so if I tether him to the desk he should be quiet."

"Oh! all right," he replied peevishly, "but make him stop this noise."

So with a piece of string I tethered the ferret to the desk which stood in front of the class.

Nelson proceeded to run around in circles and everyone thought what a wonderfully unique diversion it was to have a tame polecat cutting capers in a French lesson and roared their approval of the performance.

"I can't have this," said Sark. "Get this — this animal out of here at once."

"But I can't let him loose on his own, he might do damage," I replied.

"Well, you'll have to stay out with him."

I left the room, leading Nelson like a little dog on a leash and order was once more restored.

Our away rugby matches with other grammar and public schools were usually lively affairs, both during the games and afterwards. Two incidents connected with the games in Cardiff stick in my mind.

Our normal mode of transport to Cardiff was the train, but once the Head's son, Hue, managed to persuade his father to let him have his Austin Seven for the day. A party of four, including myself, were to travel by car. It was a miracle that we ever reached halfway to our destination as the car was pushed to its limit. Down a steep hill, we reached sixty miles an hour, with the sturdy little box on wheels swaying perilously from side to side.

At this time I was entranced by a girl in Cardiff and it was arranged that I would spend the evening at her home while the others went out on the town. I gave them the address where they could call for me, which they would do around nine-thirty.

We were left alone in the front lounge. Time flies for young people who imagine that they have each found their heart's desire, and nine-thirty came and went. At around ten o'clock we were aroused from an amorous embrace by a commotion going on in the quiet road outside. A car was roaring up and down and we could hear loud voices drifting nearer and then becoming fainter. We peeped through the curtains and saw one Austin Seven passing by with three heads poking out of the windows, lustily yelling, "TC, where are you?"

It appeared that my companions had remembered the name of the road but not the house number. We then set off, stopped to collect some fish and chips on the way, and eventually reached home without further incident.

On another occasion after a Saturday match I had arrived at our local railway station at around ten o'clock at night. My road home took me past the churchyard. It skirted two sides of it and huge dark yew trees overhung the road. A very pale moon was shining and a slight mist hung over the ground. All was intensely quiet save for the sound of my footsteps and the occasional hoot of an owl, since there was very little traffic then to disturb the quiet of the countryside.

As I neared the church I could see the tombstones, ghostlike in the moonlight, and my steps began to quicken. Then — was my imagination running away with me or did I really hear a clanking noise coming from the churchyard? No, there was something strange happening!

I glanced through the little swing gate and quickened my pace almost to a run. I had gone some twenty yards or so when I stopped. I had to find out what this was or it would be a mystery ever after. This situation might never arise again and I would always be wondering about it.

I turned back, and when I reached the little gate I almost froze on the spot, for coming along the path through the mist was a ghostly figure, making no sound and having no identity. After what seemed like an age the figure resolved itself into the caretaker, who had been to the church to stoke up the boiler to warm the church for the next day's services. With great relief I realised that I had solved the mystery and I walked most of the way home with him talking incessantly.

The last autumn term of my stay at the school a small group of us, now sixth formers and prefects, were chatting in the library and we decided that, as there were no festivities at Christmas, we should do something about it. Accordingly we sent Hue to ask his father if we would be allowed to put on an end-of-term concert.

Permission was promptly given and we eagerly set about organising talent, props, music and stage. There was no lack of volunteers, in fact everyone wanted to get in on the act. We had several quite brilliant fellows in our mob at that time. One, whom we called Shaver, had a mop of red hair which he had let grow almost to his shoulders and looked more like a girl than a boy. He played for the first fifteen and was a kind of fifth column, for when one of the opposing side saw him with the ball, he momentarily held back, no doubt thinking it would be indecent to tackle a girl, and, anyway, what was a girl doing playing for a boys' grammar school?

I was in a sketch with Shaver in which I had to shave him and sing a barber's song at the same time.

> With lather and brush,
> My days are all rush,
> I'm Suds the barber's boy . . .

Our first ventures in the field of theatrical activities went off so well that a group of four of us decided that we would put the show on in a village hall just outside the town. We didn't realise at the time what was involved. There was the hall to hire; the hall didn't have a piano, so that had to be hired, transported to the hall, and then tuned. There were tickets to have printed and entertainment tax to be sorted out and royalties to pay as this was not to be a charitable performance but a profit-making affair and we four were going to take the profits. As it turned out, I think we made about six shillings each despite having a packed audience. However, I would willingly have paid six shillings for the fun and experience which we got out of it.

On the night of the performance the hall was packed, all seats having been sold and some people were even standing at the back of the hall. My father, Hal and my girl friend from Cardiff came to see the show. In the front row sat the spiritual and temporal leader of the community in the form of the vicar.

Just before the show was due to start, Shaver suggested a slight alteration to one of his sketches, the object of which was to take the mickey, in quite a harmless way, out of our compère. Ginger didn't take kindly to this and objected strongly.

"That would be a reflection on my character," he protested.

"Don't be daft, Ginger, it's only a bit of fun," said Shaver.

"No, I don't agree. If you insert those remarks I shall walk on to the stage and tell you what I think of it in front of the audience. I mean this."

"OK — don't fuss," said Shaver.

When this particular scene came on, Shaver produced his amendment. Ginger, furious and true to his word, stalked on and angrily set about Shaver. The audience roared its approval and thought the acting most professional, not realising that it was in earnest.

One of our rugby team, a six-foot, broad-shouldered fellow, sang one of the hits of the day, "They're tough, mighty tough in the west". During his song he had to draw a six-shooter and fire a blank cartridge. The noise of this explosion in the small hall was deafening and the effect on the vicar was startling. He literally jumped from his seat and the poor man looked as though he would have apoplexy at any moment.

News of our efforts had reached certain dignitaries in the town and they asked us if we would do a couple of shows for charitable causes. This we gladly did and I'm sure we would have been happy to have done a London season if we had been asked!

My paternal grandmother wanted me to go on to university to study pharmacy, with the object of having my own business, but I was quite adamant that it was time that I began to earn a living. I had applied for a post as an analyst in the chemical laboratories of a large integrated steelworks then being built in Monmouthshire, had had an interview with the Chief Chemist and had been accepted for the post, which would become available in a few months' time. War clouds were gathering on the horizon and I was not to start reading for a degree until some seven years later.

My time at this school were some of the happiest years of my life. We were all comrades — boys and masters alike. Despite our youthful exuberance we were gradually moulded into responsible beings of character and initiative.

I always feel a debt of gratitude to these masters for their understanding and guidance, not least Neddy, whose handling of delicate situations was masterly, putting them in their correct perspective.

And now the great, wide world lay ahead of us.

Also available in ISIS Large Print:

Yabbadabbadoo

Joan Belk

"This was our secret password which we had used for years. If he looked at a picture and liked it, Albert would say, 'Yabbadabbadoo, love?' and I would answer back the same, and then we would have a good laugh."

Born in Rotherham in the 1920s, Joan's family was full of enterprising spirits. Her father sold toffees to fellow miners, while her mother made ice cream for the shop they ran from their front room. Joan herself started working at 14, before leaving to join the Air Force during the War.

Her first marriage was an unhappy one, but she had a long and contented life with her second husband, Albert. Over the years, she turned her hand to a number of jobs, from running her own shop to working in a bank, supported by Albert all the way.

ISBN 0-7531-9356-6 (hb)
ISBN 0-7531-9357-4 (pb)

Country Boy

Colin Miller

"My childhood, especially during and soon after the war, was a delightful experience that I look back on with great affection and all of my family, not just my parents, made that possible."

Colin Miller was born in 1940 in Rollesby, a village near Great Yarmouth. In Rollesby, as in so many other rural communities at this time, drinking water was drawn from a well, the lavatory was a bucket in an outside privy, transport was a bicycle or a bus, and entertainment was provided by the radio, whist drives at the village hall or a rare visit to the cinema. As the 1940s and '50s progressed, this way of life changed dramatically — some would say disappeared. Colin Miller chronicles these developments through the eyes of a Norfolk schoolboy and teenager.

ISBN 0-7531-9358-2 **(hb)**
ISBN 0-7531-9359-0 **(pb)**